THE
NUREMBERG
TRIALS

THE
NUREMBERG
TRIALS

BRINGING THE LEADERS OF
NAZI GERMANY TO JUSTICE
THE ORIGINAL TRANSCRIPTS

TERRY BURROWS

Picture credits

16 Art Media/Print Collector/Getty Images; 23 Hulton Archive/Getty Images; 40 FPG/Getty Images; 78 Library of Congress/Getty Images; 94 Fox Photos/Hulton Archive/Getty Images; 121 Galerie Bilderwelt/Getty Image; 133 Mondadori via Getty Images; 137 Roger Viollet via Getty Images; 141 Margaret Bourke-White/The LIFE Picture Collection via Getty Images/Getty Images; 151 George Skadding/The LIFE Picture Collection via Getty Images/Getty Images; 157 Kurt Hutton/Picture Post/Getty Images; 167 Keystone/Getty Images; 171 Keystone/Hulton Archive/Getty Images; 179 Fox Photos/Getty Images; 197 Keystone/Getty Images; 213 Keystone/Getty Images; 220 Fred Ramage/Getty Images; 228 Keystone/Hulton Archive/Getty Images; 249 Keystone/Getty Images; 252 Keystone/Getty Images.

This edition published in 2021 by Arcturus Publishing Limited
26/27 Bickels Yard, 151–153 Bermondsey Street,
London SE1 3HA

Copyright © Arcturus Holdings Limited

AD006711UK

Printed in the UK

Contents

INTRODUCTION:

The New Rules of Warfare

'There were, I suppose, three possible courses: to let the atrocities which had been committed go unpunished; to put the perpetrators to death or punish them by executive action; or to try them. Which was it to be? Was it possible to let such atrocities go unpunished? ... It will be remembered that after the First World War alleged criminals were handed over to be tried by Germany, and what a farce that was!'

Geoffrey Lawrence, Lord Oaksey, Main British Judge,
International Military Tribunal, Nuremberg, 1946

In an era of rapidly evolving military technology, the conference that was convened at The Hague in the Netherlands in 1899 saw the international community come together in a noble effort to codify a list of 'rules' for waging war. Over the course of two months, representatives from the 26 nations at the conference failed in their primary objective, which was to prevent the expansion of armed forces and reduce the deployment of new armaments. They did, however, manage to agree on a set of conditions for waging war on land and sea, including declarations outlawing the use of asphyxiating gases, certain types of bullet and the deployment of explosives or projectiles from hot-air balloons. (This was, remember, four years before the Wright Brothers achieved the first powered air flight.) The declarations and conventions they adopted took the form of an international treaty called the Hague Convention.

US President Theodore Roosevelt proposed that a second conference be convened in 1907. Attended this time by 44 states, once again no specific agreement could be reached on arms limitations, but there were further refinements of the convention regarding the 'rights and duties' of nations in conflict. There was no consensus on how violations among the signatories would be treated, however, other than a general view that war crimes should not go unpunished.

A third convention at The Hague had been planned for 1914, and rescheduled for 1915, but it found itself outpaced by the swift unravelling of Europe's delicate peace treaties and the outbreak of the First World War. One of the deadliest conflicts in history, during four bloody years an estimated 11 million military personnel lost their lives and a further 23 million were wounded in action. The war also ravaged the civilian populations of Western Europe, with around 8 million dead, mainly from war-related famine and disease. Hostilities ended in 1918, with Germany and its allies – Austria-Hungary, Bulgaria and the Ottoman Empire – defeated and demoralized.

Many of the terms of the Hague Conventions were violated in the course of the war – and by all sides of the conflict. Imperial Germany inflicted what became known as the 'Rape of Belgium', invading the country without explicit warning and committing mass atrocities against its civilians; Britain committed war crimes in the deliberate killing of shipwreck survivors following the sinking of German submarines *U-27* and *U-41*; and the Russian Empire was guilty of crimes against humanity on a grand scale through the massacre of Turkish and Kurdish civilians. All sides deployed chemical weapons during the fighting in the trenches of the Western Front: chlorine and mustard gases were widely used as 'irritants', with deadly phosgene gas – first used by French forces in 1915 – responsible for the vast majority of the 90,000 deaths attributable to chemical warfare.

The Treaty of Versailles

The peace settlement that followed was without precedent. For the first time in a major conflict, the victors were able to claim financial reparations from the vanquished. Furthermore, territories were seized and demands were made for the extradition of individuals accused of committing violations of both the Hague Conventions and earlier Geneva Conventions, during their treatment of wounded or captive military personnel and civilians. The Treaty of Versailles, signed in 1919, required Germany to formally 'accept responsibility' for 'all the loss and damage' inflicted on the Allies during the conflict. This was initially assessed as 132 billion marks – the equivalent of £284 billion ($442 billion) in the 21st century. There was widespread disagreement among the Allies as to the harshness of this figure. Marshal Foch of France considered it far too lenient – unsurprising, perhaps, given the carnage inflicted on his land – while British economist John Maynard Keynes called it a brutal 'Carthaginian Peace' and believed it would eventually prove counter-productive.

With the forced abdication of Kaiser Wilhelm II, post-war Germany held its first democratic elections, creating what became known as the Weimar Republic. However, the new government had little choice but to sign up to the terms of Versailles. Beyond the reparation payments, the Allied powers – Britain, France, Italy, the United States and Japan – demanded, first and foremost, the arrest of the former Kaiser as a war criminal. A distant cousin of Queen Wilhelmina of the Netherlands, 'Kaiser Bill' had been granted asylum by the Dutch government in 1918. As he was residing in a neutral state he could not be extradited, in spite of all diplomatic efforts, and the issue was eventually dropped.

In February 1920 the Allies submitted to the Weimar government a list of 900 names of individuals accused of committing war crimes, but they resisted the extradition demands, proposing instead that they should be allowed to stage prosecutions on home soil according to their own legal systems. The Allied leaders accepted and in May 1920 produced a vastly reduced list of the 45 most significant names to be sent for trial.

Staged between 23 May and 16 July 1921 at the Reichsgericht in Leipzig, Germany's supreme criminal and civil court, the trials were universally regarded as a travesty. Many of the 45 individuals accused could not be traced and went untried; in the end only a dozen faced prosecution, of whom six were found guilty of mistreating prisoners of war. They were each jailed for less than a year. Even the most serious charge of war crimes on the high seas did not attract heavy punishment; two submarine officers who had machine-gunned the survivors of a sunken Canadian hospital ship only received four-year sentences.

Needless to say, little regard was given to violations of the Hague Conventions by the Allies.

The rise of the National Socialists

How far the Treaty of Versailles and the subsequent collapse of the German economy contributed to the rise of Adolf Hitler and the Nazi Party remains a point of debate among historians. The terms of the agreement were certainly humiliating. Germany was cowed into an admission of national culpability, valuable industrial and agricultural territories were seized and its military was reduced to a fraction of its former glory. Added to that, the heavy financial burden placed on the Weimar government made economic recovery all but impossible. Since reparations had to be made in gold (of which Germany now held almost none) or hard currency, the government began the mass printing of banknotes in order to buy foreign currency. This quickly led to hyperinflation on a surreal scale: famously, a loaf of bread costing 160 marks at the end of 1922 would cost 200 billion marks a year later. The German economy gradually became more stable following the acceptance of America's Dawes Plan, which provided investments and loans that enabled reparation payments to be made. But this came at a price: with Germany's wealth tied to the American economy, the Great Depression that began with the Wall Street Crash of 1929 left both economies in ruins. By 1932 almost a third of Germany's workforce were unemployed.

It was this environment of deprivation, resentment and division that was exploited ruthlessly – and effectively – by the Nationalsozialistische Deutsche Arbeiterpartei (National Socialist German Workers' Party) and their leader, Adolf Hitler. An Austrian-born corporal in the Bavarian infantry, Hitler had been wounded at the Battle of the Somme in October 1916. Shocked and outraged by the manner of Germany's eventual capitulation, Hitler became an obsessive believer of the so-called '*Dolchstoßlegende*' ('stab-in-the-back myth'). This was an idea – popular in right-wing circles at the end of the war – that the empire had been defeated less by Allied military might than by betrayal on the home front by Bolsheviks, Jews and those republicans who had supported the downfall of Germany's monarchy.

During Hitler's ascendancy in the 1920s he declared that the Weimar government were shameful traitors who had acceded too easily to the demands of the Allied victors. Imprisoned following the failed Munich 'Beer Hall Putsch' in 1923, Hitler wrote what became the de facto handbook of the National Socialists: *Mein Kampf* ('My Struggle'). At its heart was what he saw as the twin evils of the modern world: communism and Judaism. He identified the Jews and the Bolsheviks as racially and ideologically inferior to the 'Aryan' Germans. Critical to his country's future, he believed, was the unification of all German-speaking peoples into one Pan-Germanic 'Reich' and central to that process was the expulsion of the Jews from Germany – voluntarily or otherwise. He further declared his intention to demolish Germany's parliamentary system – the Weimar government, he maintained, was working primarily for the interests of 'the Jewish peril'.

When *Mein Kampf* was published in 1925 it garnered little interest among the general public. At that time, of course, there was little to suggest that within eight years the National Socialists (referred to in English as the 'Nazis') would win control of Germany, nor that Adolf Hitler would demand and receive the supreme dictatorial powers to pursue his vision. By July 1933, however, all other political parties had been declared illegal and three months later Hitler withdrew Germany from the League of Nations – the precursor to the United Nations – and began the rapid rearmament of the military. In March 1936, in stark violation of the terms of the Treaty of Versailles, German troops reoccupied and militarized the Rhineland territory. This action won Hitler the respect of many Germans and would play a key strategic role at the start of the Second World War. Then in March 1938 Hitler took the first steps towards creating his Greater Germany when he announced the *Anschluss* – the annexation of his Austrian homeland. His arrival in the capital city of Vienna was greeted by a cheering crowd of almost a quarter of a million and he described the province as the 'newest bastion of the German Reich'.

The persecution of the half-a-million Jews who lived in Germany had begun from the time the Nazis came to power. On 1 April 1933 Hitler declared a boycott of Jewish businesses. Windows were daubed with Star of David symbols and anti-Semitic slogans and members of the Sturmabteilung (SA) – the Nazi Party's original paramilitary organization – stood menacingly outside Jewish-owned shops and the officers of doctors and lawyers, preventing entry. A week later the first overtly anti-Semitic laws were passed. Civil service employment was restricted to 'Aryan' Germans, thus preventing Jews from working in government positions or as teachers, professors, doctors or judges and literature by Jewish authors was effectively 'purged', becoming the subject of many infamous book-burning events aimed at works deemed to be 'Un-German'.

The marginalization of Jews under the Nazis was further legally defined with the enactment of the two Nuremberg Laws in September 1935: the Law for the Protection of German Blood and German Honour prohibited marriage or sexual relationships between Aryan Germans and Jews and the Reich Citizenship Law declared that Jews would be stripped of their citizenship and civil rights. This new legislation had a catastrophic impact on the Jewish population, who became increasingly excluded from German society. Aryan citizens stopped visiting Jewish shops, most of which went out of business or were transferred to non-Jewish owners.

In September 1938, Hitler's intention to annex the Sudetenland – a region in the west of Czechoslovakia inhabited by more than three million German speakers – sparked an international crisis. The Munich Agreement, signed by Germany, France, Italy and Great Britain, permitted this annexation as a means of preventing the outbreak of war and Hitler declared it to be his final territorial claim. Yet on 15 March Germany mounted a full-scale invasion of Czechoslovakia. Fearing that the next move would be on Poland, on 25 August 1939 the Anglo-Polish Defence Pact was signed, guaranteeing mutual military assistance in the event of either country being attacked. Seven days later Germany launched a 'blitzkrieg' attack before swiftly occupying Poland and two days later Britain and France declared war on Germany. The Second World War had begun.

The Jewish question

By this time more than half of Germany's Jewish population had fled, mainly to America and Great Britain. But the annexation and invasion of new territories posed a further problem for the Nazis – not least, what to do with the three-and-a-half million Polish Jews. In June 1940 a plan was proposed that would see the mass deportation of European Jewry to the island of Madagascar, off the east coast of Africa. It was thought that one million Jews per year could be resettled over a four-year period, with the island being governed as a Nazi police state by the SS (Schutzstaffel). When this was found to be impossible, at the end of 1940 Hitler asked Heinrich Himmler, head of the SS, to devise an alternative plan. One of Himmler's officers, Reinhard Heydrich, first considered the deportation of the entire Jewish population to the Soviet Union for eventual use as slave labour. Since this would have necessitated the transportation of more than four million civilians through a combat zone, however, it was not considered viable. Heydrich then called a conference of government ministers and SS leaders in the Berlin suburb of Wannsee on 20 January 1942 to discuss 'Die Endlösung der Judenfrage' – 'the final solution to the Jewish question'. What was decided that day led to what was perhaps the most infamous atrocity in human history. If the Jews could not be resettled then they would have to be systematically exterminated.

The Nazis had already engaged in mass killings: Himmler himself witnessed the execution of 100 Jewish prisoners in Minsk, gunned down in front of an open grave. One of his SS officers remarked that executions on such a scale were likely to inflict irreparable psychological damage on his firing squads; although they would continue throughout the war, it was clear that a more efficient method would have to be conceived.

Thousands of detention centres – or concentration camps – were then constructed in Germany and its occupied territories. Eight of these sites were designed and constructed to accommodate mass executions.

They were the extermination camps at Auschwitz-Birkenau, Treblinka, Belzec, Chelmno, Sobibor and Majdanek in Poland; Maly Trostinets in Reichskommissariat Ostland (now Belarus); and Sajmiste in Croatia. The Nazis had used poisonous gas in 1939 as an experiment in euthanization, an official policy for the elimination of Germany's 'imperfect specimens' – namely, the physically and mentally disabled. It was viewed by officials as the least troublesome and most efficient method of extermination. On a smaller scale, 'mobile' gas chambers were fitted inside innocuous-looking vans capable of exterminating up to 25 victims at a time. Carbon monoxide gas was used in most locations, although at Auschwitz, the largest and most notorious of the Nazi extermination camps, a form of hydrogen cyanide called Zyklon B was pumped into the gas chambers. The result was an agonizing death that could take up to 20 minutes.

Although the vast majority of the victims of the Nazi extermination camps were Jews, other minorities – Romani, Slavs, communists, Catholics and homosexuals – were among their number. In all, between 1941 and 1944 more than three million perished, among them an estimated 90 per cent of Poland's Jewish population.

How much ordinary Germans knew about this genocide remains a controversial issue. From the time the Nazis came to power in 1933 through to 'Kristallnacht' ('Crystal Night') – the tacitly supported pogrom that saw Jewish-owned shops, buildings and synagogues torched and destroyed on the night of 9 November 1938 – the official Nazi policy against the Jews had been unequivocally hostile. But how much was known about the systematic murder of the millions of Jews that took place during the war years?

Although the existence of the extermination camps had not been known to the Allies until close to the end of the war, United Nations documents made public in 2017 indicate that as early as December 1942 the US, UK and Soviet governments had been aware that at least two million German and Polish Jews had been murdered and many millions more were at risk.

These terrible atrocities only became widely known throughout the world with the harrowing film footage taken of the liberation of the concentration camps by Allied troops marching on Berlin in 1945. But as shocking as the brutal images of mass graves and emaciated corpses might have been, in the main these were not the victims of the gas chambers – most of them had died as a result of their appalling treatment at the hands of their captors or from typhoid and other diseases.

From as early as May 1942, the Nazis had taken steps to mask the true extent of the horror of the extermination camps. A covert SS group known as *Sonderaktion* 1005 was deployed to hide evidence of mass murder. This was less of an issue at the Auschwitz and Majdanek camps, where on-site furnace rooms were used to cremate the bodies of the two million who perished. At other sites, mass graves were exhumed by '*Leichenkommandos*' ('corpse units') and the bodies incinerated. By 1944, when the war on the Eastern Front had been lost and the Soviet Red Army was advancing into German territory, Nazi leaders realized that if they survived they would be held accountable for their actions. As a result, the grave 'cleaning' operations in Poland moved on apace and attempts were made to dismantle the camps themselves, using prisoners as slave labour. Many of the official records were destroyed at the same time. Only the Majdanek camp was captured largely intact during the Soviet advance through Poland towards Germany.

The fall of the Nazis

The Second World War was unequivocally the consequence of German aggression. Germany's attacking forces made rapid progress for the first two years of the war. On the Western Front the formidable Nazi military machine made its way through the Netherlands, Belgium and France and north into Norway and from the east it headed into the Soviet Union, with the expectation of a swift victory. The so-called Axis powers – Germany, Italy and Japan – also waged war in North Africa, Asia and the Pacific. But the failures began to mount up after the Nazis' first great defeat at Stalingrad and by the end of 1943 it was evident that Germany and its allies were losing the war on all fronts.

In Europe, Paris was liberated from the Nazis in August 1944 and Allied troops pushed towards Berlin from the west. Soviet forces, meanwhile, freed their own occupied territories and marched on Berlin from the east. Defeat for the Nazis was only a matter of time.

On 7 May 1945, at Reims, France, General Alfred Jodl, the German Chief of Staff (left of picture) is being presented with the document confirming Germany's unconditional surrender to the Allies.

On 29 April 1945, while holed up in the Führerbunker, his air raid shelter close to the Reich Chancellery, Adolf Hitler married his long-term mistress Eva Braun. A day later, with Red Army tanks already on the streets of Berlin, Hitler put a gun to his head and his new wife took a cyanide capsule. In accordance with his wishes, their bodies were burned together in the Chancellery gardens.

With the Führer gone, the end came quickly. Within a week Germany's generals had surrendered to the Allies. The final ceasefire came on 8 May 1945 – 'Victory in Europe Day'.

The war in the Pacific continued to rage for three further months, the Allies forcing Japan into retreat. Facing certain defeat, and with no access to food and supplies, Japan's military leaders nevertheless refused to surrender. Warned by his advisors that any attempt to invade Japan would result in catastrophic American casualties, President Harry Truman ordered the use of a devastating new weapon to hasten the end of the conflict. On 6 August 1945 US Airforce Boeing B-29 Enola Gay unleashed the first atomic device to be used in warfare. One single bomb destroyed Hiroshima, killing more than a third of the city's population. With Japan's military leaders still refusing to concede defeat, three days later a second atomic bomb was dropped, this time on the city of Nagasaki. The following day, Japan finally acquiesced and the Second World War was over. In all, it had cost the lives of more than 20 million military personnel and 40 million civilians.

In the immediate aftermath of war, Germany as a state ceased to exist. Its infrastructure and economy had collapsed, there was an acute shortage of food and Allied bombing had destroyed almost a quarter of the country's housing. The occupying forces – the United States, France, Britain and the Soviet Union – split Germany between them, each administering one of four zones; the capital city, Berlin, which was in the Soviet zone, was also subdivided into four zones.

The division of Germany would have incalculable repercussions on the global political landscape for the next half a century, with tensions between the Soviet Union and the West escalating throughout that period. In 1949 the three western zones were combined into a single self-governing state, the Federal Republic of Germany, known as West

Germany; the Soviet eastern zone would become a communist state – the German Democratic Republic or East Germany. They would remain segregated – in Berlin's case quite literally divided by a wall of concrete – until the fall of communism in 1990 enabled the reunification of Germany.

The fate of Germany following the fall of the Nazis may have been hampered by major differences among the Allies, but they were agreed on one issue: those responsible for some of the most heinous atrocities in human history would have to be held to account.

CHAPTER 1

A Basis for Trial

Although the war was far from over in October 1943, the tide by this time had turned against Hitler. The Red Army had stopped the Nazi advance into the Soviet Union with a crucial victory at Stalingrad, the US Navy began pushing back the invading Japanese in the Pacific, the Axis forces had been defeated in North Africa and Italy had surrendered. With victory in sight, between October and November 1943 the foreign ministers of Britain, the United States, China and the Soviet Union met at the Kremlin to discuss matters concerning the ending of the war. A four-part document known as the Moscow Declaration was the result.

The Four-Nation Declaration was a statement of the Allies' determination 'to continue hostilities against those Axis powers with which they respectively are at war until such powers have laid down their arms on the basis of unconditional surrender'.

Declarations were made relating to the future of Italy and Austria:

'Allied policy toward Italy must be based upon the fundamental principle that Fascism and all its evil influence and configuration shall be completely destroyed and that the Italian people shall be given every opportunity to establish governmental and other institutions based on democratic principles.'

Specifically, it further declared that: 'Fascist chiefs and army generals known or suspected to be war criminals shall be arrested and handed over to justice.'

The Allies agreed that: 'Austria, the first free country to fall a victim to Hitlerite aggression, shall be liberated from German domination.' They also fired a warning: 'Austria is reminded, however, that she has a responsibility, which she cannot evade, for participation in the war at the side of Hitlerite Germany, and that in the final settlement account will inevitably be taken of her own contribution to her liberation.'

The final part of the Moscow Declaration was its most significant, and was issued with the signatures of President Franklin Roosevelt, Prime Minister Winston Churchill and Premier Josef Stalin. The Declaration on German Atrocities gave warning that when the Nazis had been defeated the perpetrators of war crimes would be pursued ruthlessly.

'The United Kingdom, the United States and the Soviet Union have received from many quarters evidence of atrocities, massacres and cold-blooded mass executions which are being perpetrated by Hitlerite forces in many of the countries they have overrun and from which they are now being steadily expelled. The brutalities of Nazi domination are no new thing, and all peoples or territories in their grip have suffered from the worst form of government by terror. What is new is that many of the territories are now being redeemed by the advancing armies of the liberating powers, and that in their desperation the recoiling Hitlerites and Huns are redoubling their ruthless cruelties. This is now evidenced with particular clearness by monstrous crimes on the territory of the Soviet Union which is being liberated from Hitlerites, and on French and Italian territory …

'… Those German officers and men and members of the Nazi party who have been responsible for or have taken a consenting part in the above atrocities, massacres and executions will be sent back to the countries in which their abominable deeds were done in order that they may be judged and punished according to the laws of these liberated countries and of free governments which will be erected therein …

'... Germans who take part in wholesale shooting of Polish officers or in the execution of French, Dutch, Belgian or Norwegian hostages of Cretan peasants, or who have shared in slaughters inflicted on the people of Poland or in territories of the Soviet Union which are now being swept clear of the enemy, will know they will be brought back to the scene of their crimes and judged on the spot by the peoples whom they have outraged.

'Let those who have hitherto not imbrued their hands with innocent blood beware lest they join the ranks of the guilty, for most assuredly the three Allied powers will pursue them to the uttermost ends of the earth and will deliver them to their accusers in order that justice may be done.'

There may have been a clear, unequivocal desire for justice to be served but as yet there was no consensus as to what form that should take. During a dinner meeting at the Tehran Conference, barely a month after signing the Moscow Declaration, Soviet premier Stalin put forward his proposal that 50,000 German military officers should be executed. Thinking that Stalin was making a joke, President Roosevelt suggested that 49,000 would probably be sufficient. Churchill failed to see the humour and denounced what he saw as 'the cold-blooded execution of soldiers who fought for their country' – even if they had been the enemy.

Further discussions took place at the conferences of Yalta – prior to the end of the war – and Potsdam, following the surrender of Germany. Participants had once again been the Allied 'Big Three' – the United States, Britain and the Soviet Union. Within a broader framework of agreements, the leaders reached a consensus on a format for the punishment of war criminals, the legal basis of which was to be discussed at the London Conference, starting on 26 June 1945. There was also, finally, an acknowledgement that liberated France should be given a formal role in the prosecution process, as President de Gaulle had not been invited to attend the Potsdam Conference – a slight that would cause a good deal of future resentment.

Finding the major war criminals

On 1 May 1945, the day after Adolf Hitler's suicide, naval chief Admiral Karl Dönitz announced his appointment as successor to the Führer. With Berlin fallen, the new president set up a government at his naval headquarters at Flensburg in the north of Germany, close to the Danish border. Realizing that the war was lost in all but name, he devoted his brief time in office to ensuring that German forces were able to surrender in relative safety and, above all, avoid capture by Soviet troops, whom he feared would be set on exacting their own retribution.

During 4 and 5 May 1945, Dönitz ordered the ceasefire of all German forces in Europe and authorized General Alfred Jodl to sign an instrument of unconditional surrender to the Allies. On 8 May 1945, at 23:01 Central European Time, the war in Europe officially came to an end.

By the time the war was over, Adolf Hitler and other significant figures within the Nazi regime – Himmler, Goebbels, Heydrich – were dead. Realizing their likely fate, Germany's senior surviving military and civilian leaders fled from Berlin. With Germany's infrastructure close to collapse, the Allied task of collecting those who remained was not simple, but over the months that followed a large number of prominent Nazis were captured by the military and assessed for their actions.

Franz von Papen, once the Chancellor of Germany and the man responsible for bringing Hitler to power, was caught in Westphalia in April 1945. Having feared arrest by the Gestapo he had already been on the run for the previous nine months. He was discovered by American troops while eating stew in the woods with his grandchildren.

Hermann Göring, after Hitler the most powerful figure in the Nazi Party and Supreme Commander of the Luftwaffe, handed himself over to the US Army on 6 May rather than surrender to the advancing Soviet Army – a move that almost certainly saved his life.

Pictured at the beginning of the trial are (front row, left to right) Hermann Göring (writing), Rudolf Hess, Joachim von Ribbentrop and Wilhelm Keitel, (back row) Karl Dönitz, Erich Raeder, Baldur von Schirach and Fritz Sauckel. Military police stand behind them.

Arthur Seyss-Inquart, Reich Minister for Foreign Affairs during the war, was arrested by the British Army on the Elbe Bridge in Hamburg on 7 May.

Nazi radio propagandist Hans Fritzsche, whose wartime broadcasts had earned him the name 'His Master's Voice', had been present at the Führerbunker during the final days of Hitler and propaganda minister Dr Joseph Goebbels. He handed himself over to the Soviet troops on 1 May and was then taken to the Lubianka prison in Moscow. Also discovered in Berlin were Walther Funk, Minister of Economics and former president of the Reichsbank, and Admiral Erich Raeder, ex-commander-in-chief of the German Navy, who was captured by the Red Army on 23 June. He was placed under house arrest.

On 23 May, British troops arrested Karl Dönitz and other members of the Flensburg government – Alfred Jodl, Field Marshal Wilhelm Keitel and Armaments Minister Albert Speer. Also detained at Flensburg was Alfred Rosenberg, author of the influential work of Nazi ideology, *The Myth of the Twentieth Century*, which espoused theories of Aryan racial superiority and the persecution of the Jews. Dönitz had refused him a position in his government and he was discovered hiding in a hospital room by British soldiers, as they searched for one of their most prized targets, Heinrich Himmler.

Fritz Sauckel had played a central role in the Nazi forced labour schemes. Even after capture he would continue to maintain that the workers from occupied territories who had been brought to Germany were volunteers, and that he was 'an innocent man who wronged no one'.

Prominent economist Hjalmar Schacht, long out of favour with Hitler, had spent the end of the war incarcerated at the Dachau concentration camp; liberated by the US Army in late April, he was rearrested as a war criminal a month later.

Nazi politician Dr Robert Ley, a fanatical follower of Hitler and leader of the Deutsche Arbeitsfront (German Labour Front), had introduced the *Kraft durch Freude* (Strength Through Joy) regime, promoting National Socialism to the German people. He was captured by American paratroopers on 16 May in a mountain hut in the south of Bavaria.

Germany's Foreign Minister, Joachim von Ribbentrop, was arrested by a Belgian airman near Hamburg on 14 June. Discovered in bed, he was said to have been denounced by a disgruntled former business associate. Found along with him was a letter addressed to British Prime Minister Winston Churchill, which he subsequently reported as being 'extremely lengthy and dull'.

Captured by American soldiers in Munich, as Reichsminister for the Interior Wilhelm Frick had played a central role in Nazi racial policy, in particular as a lawyer drafting anti-Jewish legislation, including the Nuremberg Laws that forbade marriage and sexual activity between Jews and Germans. Also found in Munich was Julius Streicher, publisher of the notorious anti-Semitic newspaper *Der Stürmer*.

SS General Dr Ernst Kaltenbrunner was caught after fleeing to the Altaussee mountains across the Austrian border. He was the highest-ranking surviving member of the SS that the Allies could find after the war.

Governor of Vienna Baldur von Schirach had earlier been leader of the Hitler Youth. Assumed to be dead by the Allied authorities, he surrendered to the Americans in the Tyrolean city of Schwaz in June 1945.

Adolf Hitler's personal lawyer and Governor General of Occupied Poland, Hans Frank played a central role in the mass murder of Polish Jews. He was captured by US troops in Bavaria on 4 May.

Foreign Minister until 1938, Konstantin von Neurath had been Protector of Bohemia and Moravia during the war years. He was captured by French soldiers.

The former deputy Führer of the Nazi Party, Rudolf Hess, had fought a very different war. Once a member of Hitler's devoted inner circle and among the most influential figures in the Nazi Party, in 1941, as the Nazis began struggling with their war on both the Eastern and Western Fronts, he took it upon himself to approach the British with an unauthorized offer of peace between the two nations. Setting out solo in his Messerschmitt Bf 110 on 10 May 1941, Hess ejected and parachuted safely to the ground over the east coast of Scotland when his fuel ran low, where he was arrested and held captive for the duration of the war. Outraged and betrayed, Hitler declared that Hess was to be executed if he ever returned to Germany. Hess would indeed return to Germany; on 10 October 1945 as he faced trial at Nuremberg.

Gathering the prisoners

In May 1945, the US Army's Colonel Burton C. Andrus had been assigned the position of Commandant of Prisoner of War Enclosure #32, located in the tiny Luxembourg town of Mondorf-les-Bains. Code-named 'Camp Ashcan', before the war this had been the Palace Hotel, an austere six-storey building with a grand stucco façade that was used mainly as a health retreat for those taking the waters of the town's spa. Its size and remote location made it ideal for housing the captive war criminals.

Before the arrival of the defendants, the US military stripped away all vestiges of grandeur, kitting out each room with a basic army camp bed and a straw mattress. Although the Allies had wanted the whereabouts of their prisoners to be kept secret, rumours spread to an outraged press, who began describing senior Nazi war criminals living in luxury and banqueting on the finest foods and wines.

On 16 July Andrus invited members of the press to visit Camp Ashcan, so they could tell the world that these prisoners were living in the most spartan of conditions and eating and drinking standard prisoner of war fare.

He also wanted them to see that the grounds were like any other prisoner of war camp, surrounded by barbed wire, floodlights and mounted machine-gun turrets.

Camp Ashcan was home to 52 Nazi captives. On Sunday, 12 August 1945, Colonel Andrus ordered 15 of them into two military ambulances. They were then taken under escort to Luxembourg Airport, where they boarded a pair of Douglas C-47 Skytrains bound for Nuremberg.

The London Conference

During the months immediately following the war, the Allies had begun to debate a legal basis on which the prosecution of Nazi war crimes could proceed.

Between 26 June and 2 August 1945, leading legal representatives from the United States, Britain, the Soviet Union and France met in London at Church House, Westminster. The intention was to create a set of rules and procedures by which a formal military tribunal could be conducted.

Evolving from the Moscow Declaration, the document that resulted from the London Conference was formally issued on 8 August 1945. Its official title was the London Agreement, which created the International Military Tribunal and its charter, which defined the laws and procedures by which the Nuremberg Trials were to be conducted.

Although there was considerable debate over specific definitions – what constituted a crime against humanity or war of aggression, for example – the conference formally agreed a list of 30 articles, which were grouped into seven separate sections. The first part outlined the precise make-up of what was to be termed the International Military Tribunal, now more generally known as the Nuremberg Trials.

I. Constitution of the International Military Tribunal. Articles 1 to 5 confirmed that the tribunal would consist of four members, each with an alternate. Each one would be nominated by one of the four prosecuting Allies: 'By the Government of the United States of America, the Provisional Government of the French Republic, the Government of the United Kingdom of Great Britain and Northern Ireland and the Government of the Union of Soviet Socialist Republics, there shall be established an International Military Tribunal ... for the just and prompt trial and punishment of the major war criminals of the European Axis.'

II. Jurisdiction and General Principles. Articles 6 to 13 covered the procedures governing the tribunal. It was Article 6 that outlined the nature of the crimes being tried. It declared that 'The Tribunal . . . shall have the power to try and punish persons who, acting in the interests of the European Axis countries, whether as individuals or as members of organizations, committed any of the following crimes.'

Three categories of crime were defined in Article 6.

Crimes Against Peace referred to the period from when the Nazis took power to the outbreak of war: '... planning, preparation, initiation or waging of a war of aggression, or a war in violation of international treaties, agreements or assurances, or participation in a common plan or conspiracy for the accomplishment of any of the foregoing.'

War Crimes covered: '... violations of the laws or customs of war ... murder, ill-treatment or deportation to slave labor or for any other purpose of civilian population of or in occupied territory, murder or ill-treatment of prisoners of war or persons on the seas, killing of hostages, plunder of public or private property, wanton destruction of cities, towns or villages, or devastation not justified by military necessity.'

The genocide committed by the Nazis on the Jewish population was categorized as Crimes Against Humanity: '... murder, extermination, enslavement, deportation, and other inhumane acts committed against any civilian population, before or during the war; or persecutions on political, racial or religious grounds in execution of or in connection with any crime within the jurisdiction of the Tribunal, whether or not in violation of the domestic law of the country where perpetrated.'

Personal responsibility was made implicit. Leaders, organizers and instigators would be deemed responsible for all acts performed by any persons in execution of such a plan. Similarly, Article 8 declared that even if the accused was following orders from his government or a superior it would: 'not free him from responsibility, but may be considered in mitigation of punishment.'

III. Committee for the Investigation and Prosecution of Major War Criminals. Articles 14 and 15 covered the appointment, responsibilities and duties of the chief prosecutor and his staff by each member of the tribunal.

IV. Fair Trial for Defendants. Article 16 defined the rights of the Defendant, whether representing himself or through counsel. This included the right to present evidence in support of his case or to cross-examine any prosecution witness.

V. Powers of the Tribunal and Conduct of the Trial. Articles 17 to 25 defined the way in which the tribunal was to go about its business. Following the principles of civil law established by the Allied states, trials would take place before a panel of judges rather than a jury. The course of events was defined within Article 24.

(A) The Indictment shall be read in court.

(B) The Tribunal shall ask each Defendant whether he pleads 'guilty' or 'not guilty'.

(C) The Prosecution shall make an opening statement.

(D) The Tribunal shall ask the Prosecution and the Defense what evidence (if any) they wish to submit to the Tribunal, and the Tribunal shall rule upon the admissibility of any such evidence.

(E) The witnesses for the Prosecution shall be examined and after that the witnesses for the Defense. Thereafter such rebutting evidence as may be held by the Tribunal to be admissible shall be called by either the Prosecution or the Defense.

(F) The Tribunal may put any question to any witness and to any Defendant, at any time.

(G) The Prosecution and the Defense shall interrogate and may cross-examine any witnesses and any Defendant who gives testimony.

(H) The Defense shall address the court.

(I) The Prosecution shall address the court.

(J) Each Defendant may make a statement to the Tribunal.

(K) The Tribunal shall deliver judgement and pronounce sentence.

VI. Judgement and Sentence. Articles 26 to 29 established the powers of the tribunal to deliver punishment on those found guilty. In this realm it had total control. It agreed that the reasoning behind each sentence would be given, but that this was a final decision and not subject to review. If there was any doubt about the ultimate powers of the tribunal they were made explicit in Article 27: 'The Tribunal shall have the right to impose upon a Defendant, on conviction, death or such other punishment as shall be determined by it to be just.'

VII. Expenses. Article 30 established that the costs of the International Military Tribunal were to be borne by Germany.

The Charter was issued on 8 August 1945 and was signed off by Robert Jackson for the United States government, François de Menthon for France, Sir Hartley Shawcross for Britain and General Roman Rudenko for the Soviet Union.

By this time, a venue for the International Military Tribunal had been agreed. Mainly at the behest of the Soviet Union, Berlin was initially seen as the most likely location; it was, after all, the state capital and had been the scene of Hitler's last stand. Luxembourg, as the location of the incarcerated war criminals, and the city of Leipzig, formerly one of Germany's principal legal centres, had also been considered. There were a number of reasons which made Nuremberg's Justizpalast – the Palace of Justice – the most appropriate venue for the International Military Tribunal. There was, of course, a symbolic dimension in that the city of Nuremberg was widely regarded as the true home of the Nazi Party. It was also the geographical centre of the German Reich. Nuremberg had played host to the Nazi Party's spectacular annual propaganda rallies between 1927 and 1938, the sixth Party Congress in 1934 being dramatically documented in Leni Riefenstahl's film *Triumph des Willens* (Triumph of the Will). Yet there was a more prosaic reason: the Palace of Justice was one of the few official buildings of a suitable size that had not been badly damaged by Allied bombing raids.

With a commitment to making the trials 'fair and expeditious', the first day of the Nuremberg trial of major war criminals was scheduled to begin on the morning of 20 November 1945.

Making the case against the Nazis

The charges against the defendants were to be based on the protocols set out in the London Charter, which would result in a detailed statement of the indictments that would be read out on the first day of the Tribunal. First, however, there was the trickier question of precisely which of the captive Nazis should face trial. Camp Ashcan in Luxembourg alone held 52 prominent prisoners; others were being held in Allied prison camps in other parts of Europe or the Soviet Union. If every captive were to be tried then the Tribunal might conceivably go on for years.

The British prosecutors in particular had wanted a shortlist of the most notorious figures – those most likely to be known to the public – and put forward a list of ten. The Americans considered this too small a selection. There was also some disagreement between the two countries as to whether admirals Dönitz and Raeder should be tried; the British Admiralty was of the view that when compared to other parts of the Nazi war machine the German Navy had fought a relatively fair fight.

To back up the prosecution cases a number of captive witnesses would be called to testify at Nuremberg. But it was clear that the most significant evidence was to be provided by the Nazis themselves, in the form of the vast volumes of captured official documentation. As the war began drawing to an inevitable conclusion, direct instructions had been issued from Berlin that all official archives containing government and military documentation should be destroyed. With Germany close to collapse, compliance with these orders was not always a high priority. As the Allied forces swept inland from the Western Front, British and American troops had been issued with instructions to collect official documents as they were found. Not long after the German surrender, most of the paper evidence, from the earliest days of the Nazi regime to the fall of Hitler, was in the hands of the Allies.

A rich source of incriminating material from the German Foreign Ministry was discovered in two secure locations near the Harz mountains in Lower Saxony. The archives – some 400 tonnes of paperwork – had originally been moved there from Berlin during the bombing raids of 1943. They were now taken by the US military to Schloss Marburg, an 11th-century castle fortress in Hesse, for review. The treasure trove included valuable volumes of Hitler's personal correspondence. And embarrassingly for the British royal family, there was also information suggesting that the Duke of Windsor – the former king who had abdicated in 1936 – might have been prepared to side with the Nazis and broker a British surrender in 1940, in return for his restoration to the throne.

The Nazis had archived voluminously and in impressive detail. There was correspondence from German High Command and there were official diaries, top secret military documents and complete sets of records of prisoners and guards at the Buchenwald and Nordhausen concentration camps. These 'libraries' of official documentation were studied at rapid speed at centres in Washington, Paris and London. The information would provide the prime evidence behind the indictments.

When the list of defendants was finalized it contained 24 names: Hermann Göring, Joachim von Ribbentrop, Rudolf Hess, Ernst Kaltenbrunner, Alfred Rosenberg, Hans Frank, Martin Bormann, Wilhelm Frick, Robert Ley, Fritz Sauckel, Albert Speer, Walther Funk, Hjalmar Schacht, Franz von Papen, Konstantin von Neurath, Baldur von Schirach, Arthur Seyss-Inquart, Julius Streicher, Wilhelm Keitel, Alfred Jodl, Erich Raeder, Karl Dönitz and Hans Fritzsche.

Also included among this list of Nazi officials was the name of one of Germany's most prominent industrialists, Gustav Krupp von Bohlen und Halbach. Friedrich Krupp AG, the family company he ran, had been responsible for the production of much of Germany's military might, building U-boats, battleships, tanks, infantry weapons and powerful field guns. During the war, the company had opened facilities in the occupied territories of Eastern Europe, manned largely by forced labour. Krupp's inclusion on the list had been controversial. He had initially opposed the appointment of Hitler as German Chancellor but thereafter had co-operated with the Nazis mainly as an expedient course of action for his business empire. By the end of the Second World War he was already in his mid-seventies and in increasingly poor health.

The list was published on 29 August 1945 and received lengthy comment from the world's press, who seemed – by and large – to be in agreement. By this time, the Allied legal teams had also agreed on the contents of the indictment document, which contained the four specific charges – war crimes, crimes against peace, crimes against humanity and the 'common plan' or conspiracy to commit those three crimes – that the defendants would face when the trial of the major war criminals commenced on 20 November 1945.

CHAPTER 2

The Trial of the Major War Criminals Begins

As agreed within the articles of the London Charter, each of the four prosecuting nations nominated one judge and one non-voting alternate; each also provided a prosecution team headed by a chief prosecutor.

America's primary judge was Francis Biddle, a noted legal mind who had been the United States Attorney General throughout the war. His alternate was circuit judge John J. Parker.

Clement Attlee, who had only held the post of Britain's Prime Minister since July 1945, nominated Lord Justice Colonel Sir Geoffrey Lawrence as Britain's primary judge. A figure widely respected for the clarity of his judicial pronouncements, Lawrence – later Lord Oaksey – was chosen by his peers as President of the Tribunal. His alternate, Norman Birkett, had originally been asked to take on the role but was overruled by the Foreign Office. Although he had no voting capacity, Birkett would be influential in the making of key decisions and later received wide praise for his work throughout the trial.

The Soviet Union's primary judge was Major General Iona Nikitchenko. Already a well-known international figure, he had presided over a number of Josef Stalin's show trials during the 'Great Purge' of the late 1930s – including those that saw the execution of 'counter-revolutionaries' Kamanev and Zinoviev. Often controversial, before the Tribunal had even begun Nikitchenko made it clear that as far as the Soviet Union was concerned the guilt of the accused had already been established. In his view, 'the whole idea is to secure quick and just punishment for the crime'. Indeed, he believed that any impartiality on the part of the judges 'would only lead to unnecessary delays'. His alternate was Alexander Volchkov, a film producer turned lawyer.

Henri Donnedieu de Vabres represented France's interim post-war government – the Provisional Government of the French Republic – along with his alternate, Robert Falco, one of the main authors of the London Charter. Even before the start of the war, Donnedieu, a progressive legal academic, had been an avid campaigner for the establishment of an International Criminal Court.

President Truman had granted leave of absence to the former US Attorney General, Associate Justice Robert H. Jackson, to assist in the drafting of the London Charter and to represent the United States as chief prosecutor at the International Military Tribunal. A powerful orator, Jackson's eloquent opening address is still widely studied. The American prosecution team was much the largest assembled for Nuremberg, with Jackson aided by two executive counsellors, four associates and 16 assistants.

The British prosecution was headed up by Attorney General Sir Hartley Shawcross. His opening address at Nuremberg contained the famed rebuttal on the issue of personal responsibility: 'There comes a point when a man must refuse to answer to his leader if he is also to answer to his own conscience.' Unlike others at Nuremberg, his view was that the trial should focus on war crimes that resulted from violations of international agreements rather than on exacting vengeance on the perpetrators.

Soviet lawyer Lieutenant General Roman Rudenko was Procurator-General of Ukraine and had already achieved a degree of international notoriety in June 1945 as the prosecutor at the 'Trial of Sixteen', one of Stalin's show trials that saw the imprisonment of the leaders of the post-war Polish Underground State, accused of 'illegal activity' against the Red Army. He would later be awarded the title Hero of Socialist Labour.

President De Gaulle nominated his Attorney General François de Menthon as France's chief prosecutor. He had already led the

Commission d'Épuration, rooting out those who had collaborated with the Nazis during the occupation and supervising the high-profile trial of Marshal Pétain, former head of the Vichy government. In January 1946 he resigned from the Tribunal to embark on a political career. His place was taken by veteran politician Auguste Champetier de Ribes.

In spite of a clear lack of impartiality among some of the Tribunal's senior officials, conditions had been laid out in Article 16 of the London Charter to ensure that those on trial received a fair hearing:

> 'A Defendant shall have the right to conduct his own defense before the Tribunal or to have the assistance of Counsel … or through his Counsel to present evidence at the Trial in support of his defense, and to cross-examine any witness called by the Prosecution.'

As such, each of the defendants was able to choose his own individual counsel, most of whom were prominent German civil or military lawyers. The main defence counsel were supported by a team of more than 70 lawyers, clerks and assistants.

The Nuremberg cells

Before the start of the Tribunal the defendants were held in prison cells close to the Palace of Justice in Nuremberg. Still under the command of Colonel Andrus, conditions here were very different from Camp Ashcan. Although the prisoners had once been allowed to mix and chat among themselves, they were now confined to their own cells. Andrus had made it clear from the beginning that former military or Nazi Party status now meant nothing. Once nationally-feted high-ranking men such as Göring, Papen, Ribbentrop, Dönitz and Hess bitterly resented the lack of respect they were now shown by Andrus and other Allied commanders. They had been guaranteed humane treatment but all other privileges were gone. Their cells were small, each no more than 13ft x 6ft 6in (4m x 2m), with cold, bare-cobbled floors. Furnishings were austere, consisting of nothing more than an iron bedstead with a straw mattress and standard-issue US Army blankets, a small wooden table and chair and a tiny lavatory bowl. Daily routines were initiated, with each prisoner personally responsible for cleaning his own cell. Andrus had taken the decision to allow his charges access to library books, taking the view – by no means shared by all of his colleagues – that the trial could only be hindered by defendants in the grip of cabin fever. They were also allowed 30 minutes of exercise each day in the prison yard; the only time the defendants were given the opportunity to talk among themselves.

Before and throughout the Tribunal, the prisoners were monitored by American psychologist Gustave Gilbert and psychiatrist Douglas Kelley. Gilbert, in particular, would become the confidant of a number of the prisoners, including Göring and Ribbentrop. He kept a fascinating record of his interviews and interrogations, which were published after the Tribunal had ended. Most of those on trial showed little in the way of remorse, although some of them, so Gilbert recalled, were more than indignant about their fate. Dr Robert Ley was particularly frank with his words: 'Stand us against a wall and shoot us – well and good, you are victors. But why should I be brought before a Tribunal?'

Four days after receiving his indictment on 21 October 1945, Ley fashioned a noose from torn strips of towel and hanged himself from a lavatory water tank. This was an embarrassment to Colonel Andrus and the US military, who had feared such an event. Andrus first tried to keep the news secret from the other prisoners, believing some might be inspired to follow suit, and then he quadrupled the number of guards, with one guard now allocated to each cell. The remaining prisoners – much to their irritation – would thereafter be monitored around the clock.

Gilbert and Kelley were tasked with performing ongoing psychiatric evaluations. Rudolf Hess was a particular concern, given that he had twice attempted suicide while a British prisoner of war, and was always handcuffed to a guard when he left his cell. Kelley considered Hess to be a 'paranoid and schizoid' personality, and therefore mentally unstable, but nonetheless he viewed him as fit to stand trial.

During this time, Gilbert and Kelley were able to examine 21 of the defendants held at Nuremberg, administering Rorschach inkblot and

Thematic Apperception pysychological tests and the Wechsler-Bellevue Intelligence test. The IQ tests – although open to wide interpretation – showed a set of scores well above the average, with several of the highest scorers in what some metrics would regard as the 'genius or near-genius' category: Hjalmar Schacht (143); Arthur Seyss-Inquart (141); Hermann Göring (138); Karl Dönitz (138); Franz von Papen (134); Erich Raeder (134); Dr Hans Frank (130); Hans Fritzsche (130); Baldur von Schirach (130); Joachim von Ribbentrop (129); Wilhelm Keitel (129); Albert Speer (128); Alfred Jodl (127); Alfred Rosenberg (127); Konstantin von Neurath (125); Walther Funk (124); Wilhelm Frick (124); Rudolf Hess (120); Fritz Sauckel (118); Ernst Kaltenbrunner (113); Julius Streicher (106).

The Nuremberg Trials were to be heavily reported in the media so the Allies were insistent that defendants should be made presentable for the courtroom. From their arrival in Nuremberg prisoners were allowed to bathe and shower twice weekly and were shaved by a barber every other day. When the trial of the major war criminals itself began, ablutions took place each morning before they entered the courtroom.

The Krupp controversy

The inclusion of Gustav Krupp von Bohlen und Halbach in the list of defendants had always been problematic, not least since he was almost 70 years old at the start of the war and by that time had largely handed over the running of the Krupp industrial empire to his son, Alfried. Six days before the trial was due to begin, on 14 November 1945, the Tribunal met for the first time to debate a motion brought by Dr Theodor Klefisch, Krupp's defence counsel. He submitted that medical specialists had evaluated Gustav Krupp as too ill to face trial.

'He can only speak a few disconnected words now and again, and during the last two months has not even been able to recognize his relatives and friends. On the basis of these facts one can only establish that Krupp has no knowledge of the serving of the Indictment of 19 October. Thus he does not know that he is accused and why.'

Part of the Krupp Essen gun factory, pictured around 1940.

America's chief counsel, Robert H. Jackson, opposed the motion: 'We represent three nations of the earth, one of which has been invaded three times with Krupp armaments, one of which has suffered in this war in the East as no people have ever suffered under the impact of war.'

Jackson agreed to the motion so long as Krupp's son, Alfried, be placed on a supplementary indictment. At that time under British arrest, Alfried Krupp was arguably a more legitimate target, but following a heated debate with Tribunal President Lord Justice Lawrence the request was denied.

The following day the court made its decision, based on the findings of its own appointed medical commission. Krupp suffered, the five doctors concurred, 'from senile softening of the brain ... his mental condition is such that he is incapable of understanding court procedure and of understanding or cooperating in interrogations ... and that his condition is unlikely to improve but rather will deteriorate further.'

A request for Krupp to be tried *in absentia* was granted only if during the trial it was found to be 'necessary in the interests of justice'.

As it happened, the elder Krupp never did face punishment. His health continued to deteriorate until his death in January 1950. However, his son Alfried would later face the court at one of the dozen 'subsequent' Nuremberg Trials, where in 1948 he was found guilty of using slave labour. Imprisoned for 12 years, he received a pardon three years later.

Court procedure

The proceedings at the Nuremberg Trials would naturally have to be conducted in English, French, Russian and German, and all of its official documentation would have to appear in the same four languages. Unsurprisingly, this would create considerable logistical problems in both the translation of preparatory paperwork and the 'real-time' translation of every word spoken at the Tribunal. Indeed, it would be the first time that 'simultaneous interpretation' had been used on such a scale. In previous international conferences one party would talk and then stop and wait while the interpreter translated for the other party. However, the International Military Tribunal had been created with a deliberate sense of urgency – it had been decided that the proceedings should be 'expeditious' – which necessitated speeding up the translation process between the four languages.

Colonel Léon Dostert, a French foreign language expert working for the US Army, was asked to lead the interpretation systems at the Tribunal. Using equipment newly developed by IBM, Dostert conceived the idea of simultaneous translation, where the interpreter listened through a headset and at the same time gave a translation into a separate microphone. It was a hugely demanding new skill but without it the Tribunal would have taken many months longer and would have been even more arduous for those involved. Heading three teams of a dozen translators, Dostert's innovation allowed the trial to be broadcast simultaneously in English, French, Russian and German – and enabled anyone in the courtroom to hear the proceedings in the language of their choosing.

The opening day

On the morning of Tuesday, 20 November 1945, the International Military Tribunal began its first session. Security at this point was of paramount concern. Fears – however unfounded – had persisted that Nazi sympathizers might attempt some kind of rescue of the defendants or even launch an armed attack on the courtroom. Soldiers and military policemen were placed in the maze of corridors surrounding the court and anyone attending the hearings was searched and obliged to show an official pass before being allowed to enter. Outside the building, five American M24 light-armour tanks were manned ready for action.

The commencement date of the Tribunal had only been finally confirmed during the previous day. All four of the prosecution teams had worked under extreme pressure, each facing their own difficulties during the preparation of their cases. Matters of government legislation had meant that Britain's chief prosecutor, Sir Hartley Shawcross, had only been able to join his team six days earlier, so the content of his opening speech had been left in the hands of his assistants, Mervyn Griffith Jones and Major Sir David Maxwell Fyfe. The Americans, too, rushed to have their trial briefs prepared and distributed in time. Nonetheless, like the British, they maintained that they were ready to begin.

Much to the chagrin of the judges, determined that such a high-profile trial should be executed as smoothly as possible, Russia and France pushed for a postponement. On the surface, the Soviet team had a reasonable case: they had asked for a 12-day delay on the grounds that chief prosecutor Rudenko had contracted malaria. There were also practical problems attached to having the vast number of trial documents translated and duplicated in time, although the Soviet prosecutors had already been lent translators, typewriters and duplicating equipment by the British team. The French prosecutors also called for a postponement while they argued small points of procedure, but observers generally considered this to be a ruse to buy additional preparation time.

Ignoring the postponement requests, the judges insisted that the Tribunal would begin as planned on the following day.

The Justizpalast, or Palace of Justice, on Nuremberg's Fürther Strasse, an imposing building completed in 1916, had received little structural damage at the hands of Allied bombers during the latter years of the war. To the north of the palace stood an adjacent prison that would hold the 22 defendants. Before the commencement of the Tribunal a wooden connecting passage was built between the prison and the East Building of the palace so that the prisoners could be moved securely between their cells and the courtroom. Located on the second floor of the palace's eastern wing, Courtroom 600, with its dark, dreary wood-panelled interior, received extensive structural modifications. Walls were removed to accommodate the large numbers attending the Tribunal and the IBM transmission system used for the simultaneous language interpretation required the rewiring of the room so that every person – including the press and the public – could hear the proceedings through headsets.

The primary judges – the French, the British and the Americans in their own legal attire and the Russians in uniform reflecting their military rank – sat on a low platform beneath the windows on the west side.

The opening introduction was given by Sir Geoffrey Lawrence, who had been elected as the President of the Tribunal. His address took the form of an explicit statement of the principles on which the court had been established.

'This International Military Tribunal has been established pursuant to the Agreement of London, dated the 8th of August 1945, and the Charter of the Tribunal ... to be the just and prompt trial and punishment of the major war criminals of the European Axis.

'The Signatories to the Agreement and Charter are the Government of the United Kingdom of Great Britain and Northern Ireland, the Government of the United States of America, the Provisional Government of the French Republic, and the Government of the Union of Soviet Socialist Republics. The Committee of the Chief Prosecutors, appointed by the four Signatories, have settled the final designation of the war criminals to be tried by the Tribunal, and have approved the Indictment on which the present defendants stand charged here today.

'...The trial which is now about to begin is unique in the history of the jurisprudence of the world and it is of supreme importance to millions of people all over the globe. For these reasons, there is laid upon everybody who takes any part in this trial a solemn responsibility to discharge their duties without fear or favour, in accordance with the sacred principles of law and justice.'

Lawrence also gave a reminder to those in attendance.

'This trial is a public trial in the fullest sense of those words, and I must, therefore, remind the public that the tribunal will insist upon the complete maintenance of order and decorum, and will take the strictest measures to enforce it.'

Courtroom 600 was indeed packed, with the public gallery resembling a night at the opera, many observers achieving a better view by using binoculars. The atmosphere and sense of occasion was further heightened by the flashes of the press photographers and the noise of the film crews before the trial began. This was to be a deliberately public affair, with every second of the proceedings being recorded.

Two rows of court reporters were lined up in front of the judges, the witness box on their immediate right. Also before the judges, in a boxed-off area, sat the defendants, guarded by American military police officers – the 'snowdrops' – their bright white helmets a stark contrast to the drab surroundings. Directly in front of the box sat the defence counsel and alongside them the prosecution teams. The world's press, situated behind the prosecutors, had been allocated 235 seats. Above them were the 128 seats of the public gallery. The fact that almost everyone in the room was sporting a headset gave the proceedings a more than surreal air.

The indictment

In spite of the build-up and high expectations, the first day in court was distinctly lacking in drama as each of the names of the defendants and the four indictments were read out in the courtroom. There were no surprises here, since they had already been served on the defendants and their legal teams a month earlier.

There were 24 defendants named, along with the official bodies of which they were members. Circumstances had changed, however, since the publication of the indictments. Dr Robert Ley had hanged himself and Gustav Krupp was now deemed medically unfit to stand trial. Furthermore, Martin Bormann, Hitler's personal secretary, who had been with the Führer during his last days, was still – as far as the Tribunal was concerned – at large. With no evidence to confirm Bormann's death, the Tribunal agreed that he would be tried *in absentia*, as permitted under Article 12 of the Charter.

Sir Sydney Alderman, associate trial counsel for the United States, listed the names and organizations on trial and then proceeded with the first indictment.

'The United States of America, the French Republic, the United Kingdom of Great Britain and Northern Ireland, and the Union of Soviet Socialist Republics ... hereby accuse as guilty, in the respects hereinafter set forth, of Crimes against Peace, War Crimes, and Crimes against Humanity, and of a Common Plan or Conspiracy to commit those Crimes ... Hermann Wilhelm Göring, Rudolf Hess, Joachim von Ribbentrop, Robert Ley, Wilhelm Keitel, Ernst Kaltenbrunner, Alfred Rosenberg, Hans Frank, Wilhelm Frick, Julius Streicher, Walther Funk, Hjalmar Schacht, Gustav Krupp von Bohlen und Halbach, Karl Dönitz, Erich Raeder, Baldur von Schirach, Fritz Sauckel, Alfred Jodl, Martin Bormann, Franz von Papen, Arthur Seyss-Inquart, Albert Speer, Konstantin von Neurath and Hans Fritzsche, individually and as members of any of the following groups or organizations to which they respectively belonged, namely: Die Reichs Regierung (Reich Cabinet); Das Korps der Politischen Leiter der Nationalsozialistischen Deutschen Arbeiterpartei (Leadership Corps of the Nazi Party); Die Schutzstaffeln der Nationalsozialistischen Deutschen Arbeiterpartei (commonly known as the "SS") and including Der Sicherheitsdienst (commonly known as the "SD"); Die Geheime Staatspolizei (Secret State Police, commonly known as the "Gestapo"); Die Sturm Abteilungen der NSDAP (commonly known as the "SA"); and the General Staff and High Command of the German Armed Forces.'

The three crimes listed in Article 6 of the London Charter formed the basis of the Tribunal's four indictment counts: Crimes Against Peace, War Crimes, Crimes Against Humanity and a Common Plan or Conspiracy to commit those three crimes. One or more of four indictments would be applied to each defendant, each count to be conducted by a different representative of the four prosecuting Allies.

COUNT ONE: THE COMMON PLAN OR CONSPIRACY

The indictment began with a statement of the offence.

'All the defendants, with diverse other persons, during a period of years preceding 8 May 1945, participated as leaders, organisers, instigators, or accomplices in the formulation or execution of a Common Plan or Conspiracy to commit ... Crimes against Peace, War Crimes, and Crimes against Humanity ... and are individually responsible for their own acts and for all acts committed by any persons in the execution of such plan and conspiracy.'

The Common Plan referred to the aims of the Nazi Party, the way in which they had come to power and consolidated their hold over Germany, and ultimately: 'Planned, prepared, initiated, and waged wars of aggression, which were also wars in violation of international treaties, agreements, or assurances.'

Crimes against Peace had been committed, it noted, 'in that the defendants planned, prepared, initiated, and waged wars of aggression, which were also wars in violation of international treaties, agreements, or assurances'.

The indictment continued to describe how War Crimes were carried out in pursuit of the Common Plan, stating that the defendants:

'Contemplated ... determined upon and carried out, ruthless wars against countries and populations, in violation of the rules and customs of war, including as typical and systematic means by which the wars were prosecuted, murder, ill-treatment, deportation for slave labour and for other purposes of civilian populations of occupied territories, murder and ill-treatment of prisoners of war and of persons on the high seas, the taking and killing of hostages, the plunder of public and private property, the wanton destruction of cities, towns, and villages, and devastation not justified by military necessity.

'The Common Plan or Conspiracy contemplated and came to embrace as typical and systematic means, and the defendants determined upon and committed, Crimes against Humanity, both within Germany and within occupied territories, including murder, extermination, enslavement, deportation, and other inhumane acts committed against civilian populations before and during the war, and persecutions on political, racial, or religious grounds, in execution of the plan for preparing and prosecuting aggressive or illegal wars, many of such acts and persecutions being violations of the domestic laws of the countries where perpetrated.'

The indictment further outlined the way in which the Nazi Party was central to the achievement of these aims, first providing background details of its creation, common objectives and methods. The court made clear its beliefs that those who joined the Party knew its aims precisely.

'In 1921 Adolf Hitler became the supreme leader or Führer of the Nationalsozialistische Deutsche Arbeiterpartei (National Socialist German Workers' Party), also known as the Nazi Party, which had been founded in Germany in 1920. He continued as such throughout the period covered by this Indictment ... Each defendant became a member of the Nazi Party and of the conspiracy, with knowledge of their aims and purposes, or, with such knowledge, became an accessory to their aims and purposes at some stage of the development of the conspiracy. ... The aims and purposes of the Nazi Party ... were, or came to be, to accomplish the following by any means deemed opportune, including unlawful means, and contemplating ultimate resort to threat of force, force, and aggressive war.'

Three specific objectives were detailed. The first was to 'abrogate and overthrow' the restrictions on Germany's military armaments laid out in the Treaty of Versailles after the end of the First World War. Second was the intention to regain the territories lost following the war and to take control of areas deemed to be occupied principally by what the court termed 'racial Germans'. Finally, the acquisition of additional territories 'in continental Europe and elsewhere' deemed as *'Lebensraum'* or 'living space'. This idea preceded the Nazis by more than two decades. In 1897, German geographer Friedrich Ratzel had used the term to describe the significance of migration in the successful adaptation of a species. In human terms, this effectively meant one group of *'Völker'* ('peoples') conquering and colonizing another. It was a fashionable idea in early-20th-century Germany – and led to the encouragement of migration from Germany to its colonies in Africa.

By the time Hitler wrote *Mein Kampf* in 1924 he was firmly fixated on the idea that *Lebensraum* would be found by moving east, through Poland into Russia. He believed that the Bolshevik revolution had been the work of the Jews and although he had earlier argued that an alliance with Russia would be desirable 'when Jewry is removed', his intention was that Germany should take control of western Russia and that its citizens should either be used as slave labour or deported to Siberia. This was at the very heart of his decision to invade the Soviet Union in 1941.

A key component of the first indictment was laid out in what was described as 'Doctrinal techniques of the Common Plan or Conspiracy'. These were what was seen as the dissemination and exploitation of four fundamental tenets of the Nazi Party.

'That persons of so-called "German blood" were a "master race" and were accordingly entitled to subjugate, dominate, or exterminate other "races" and peoples.'

'That the German people should be ruled under the *Führerprinzip* (Leadership Principle) according to which power was to reside in a Führer from whom sub-leaders were to derive authority in a hierarchical order … and the power of the leadership was to be unlimited, extending to all phases of public and private life.'

'That war was a noble and necessary activity of Germans.'

'That the leadership of the Nazi Party, as the sole bearer of the foregoing and other doctrines of the Nazi Party, was entitled to shape the structure, policies, and practices of the German State and all related institutions, to direct and supervise the activities of all individuals within the State, and to destroy all opponents.'

The First Count of the indictment gave a detailed assessment of the manner in which Hitler and the Nazi Party acquired totalitarian political control of Germany by 'legal' forms supported by 'terrorism' and the creation and use of 'Die Sturmabteilungen (SA), a semi-military, voluntary organization of young men trained for and committed to the use of violence, whose mission was to make the Party the master of the streets'.

After Hitler became Chancellor in January 1933:

'The Nazi conspirators reduced the Reichstag to a body of their own nominees and curtailed the freedom of popular elections throughout the country ... They united the offices of the President and the Chancellor in the person of Hitler, instituted a widespread purge of civil servants, and severely restricted the independence of the judiciary and rendered it subservient to Nazi ends ... German life was dominated by Nazi doctrine and practice and progressively mobilized for the accomplishment of their aims.

'In order to make their rule secure from attack and to instil fear in the hearts of the German people, the Nazi conspirators established and extended a system of terror against opponents and supposed or suspected opponents of the regime. They imprisoned such persons without judicial process, holding them in "protective custody" and concentration camps, and subjected them to persecution, degradation, despoilment, enslavement, torture, and murder.'

When detailing the planning and intent behind the treatment of Jews, the indictment published key quotes from several of the defendants as 'typical of the declarations of the Nazi conspirators throughout the course of their conspiracy'. Robert Ley was quoted as having declared: 'We swear we are not going to abandon the struggle until the last Jew in Europe has been exterminated and is actually dead. It is not enough to isolate the Jewish enemy of mankind – the Jew has got to be exterminated.'

A similar remark was attributed to Julius Streicher: 'The sun will not shine on the nations of the earth until the last Jew is dead.'

The remainder of the First Count of the indictment presented a lengthy and detailed outline of Germany's arms build-up, its violations of treaties and agreements and its justifications for military aggression at the beginning of the war. Emphasis was placed on the preparation and planning of unprovoked military activity.

> 'The aggressive war prepared for by the Nazi conspirators through their attacks on Austria and Czechoslovakia was actively launched by their attack on Poland ... After the total defeat of Poland, in order to facilitate the carrying out of their military operations against France and the United Kingdom, the Nazi conspirators made active preparations for an extension of the war in Europe ... All these invasions had been specifically planned in advance.'

The prosecution according to Count One of the indictment would be carried out by the United States.

COUNT TWO: CRIMES AGAINST PEACE

The second count was presented to the courtroom by British prosecutor Sir David Maxwell Fyfe. He listed the 'wars of aggression' waged by the defendants and said that they 'during a period of years preceding 8 May 1945, participated in the planning, preparation, initiation, and waging of wars of aggression, which were also wars in violation of international treaties, agreements, and assurances'.

The document listed the countries against which Germany had ignited war: 'Against Poland, 1 September 1939; against the United Kingdom and France, 3 September 1939; against Denmark and Norway, 9 April 1940; against Belgium, the Netherlands, and Luxembourg, 10 May 1940; against Yugoslavia and Greece, 6 April 1941; against the U.S.S.R., 22 June 1941; and against the United States of America, 11 December 1941.'

He concluded that the defendants had violated 'international treaties, agreements, and assurances ... in the course of planning, preparing, and initiating these wars'.

COUNT THREE: WAR CRIMES

The only Nuremberg indictment to contain much in the way of detailed crimes, Count Three covered violations committed by Germany on the civilian populations of invaded territories throughout the course of the Second World War.

After a 15-minute adjournment, the court resumed with Pierre Mounier, Assistant French Prosecutor, declaring the statement of offence for the third indictment: 'All the defendants committed War Crimes between 1 September 1939 and 8 May 1945, in Germany and in all those countries and territories occupied by the German Armed Forces since 1 September 1939, and in Austria, Czechoslovakia, and Italy, and on the High Seas.'

Considerable attention was given to the nature of the war waged by the German military, in particular the brutal blitzkrieg tactic first deployed during the swift invasion of Poland in 1939:

'This plan involved, among other things, the practice of "total war" including methods of combat and of military occupation in direct conflict with the laws and customs of war, and the commission of crimes perpetrated on the field of battle during encounters with enemy armies, and against prisoners of war, and in occupied territories against the civilian population of such territories ... Throughout the period of their occupation of territories overrun by their armed forces the defendants, for the purpose of systematically terrorizing the inhabitants, murdered and tortured civilians, and ill-treated them, and imprisoned them without legal process.'

Much of Count Three focused on the 'murder and ill-treatment of civilian populations of or in occupied territory', beginning with a harrowing list of the types of violation for which evidence existed.

'Murders and ill-treatment were carried out by diverse means, including shooting, hanging, gassing, starvation, gross overcrowding, systematic under-nutrition, systematic imposition of labour tasks beyond the strength of those ordered to carry them out, inadequate provision of surgical and medical services, kickings, beatings, brutality and torture of all kinds, including the use of hot irons and pulling out of fingernails and the performance of experiments by means of operations and otherwise on living human subjects. In some occupied territories the defendants interfered in religious matters, persecuted members of the clergy and monastic orders, and expropriated church property. They conducted deliberate and systematic genocide, viz., the extermination of racial and national groups, against the civilian populations of certain occupied territories in order to destroy particular races and classes of people and national, racial, or religious groups, particularly Jews, Poles, and Gypsies and others.'

Details of specific examples were listed from the Nazi invasions of France, Belgium, Denmark, Holland, Luxembourg, the Channel Islands, Poland, Czechoslovakia and the Soviet Union. These included concentration camp victims in Germany and Eastern Europe, the arrest and torture of thousands of French citizens during the occupation and 'over 20,000 persons who were killed in the city of Leningrad by the barbarous artillery barrage and the bombings'.

The second part of the third indictment was read out by Charles Gerthoffer, another Assistant French Prosecutor, who focused on the use by the Nazis of forced labour from invaded territories.

'It was the policy of the German Government and of the German High Command to deport able-bodied citizens from such occupied countries to Germany and to other occupied countries for the purpose of slave labour upon defense works, in factories, and in other tasks connected with the German war effort.'

This was a clear violation not only of the Hague Convention but also of 'the laws and customs of war, the general principles of criminal law as derived from the criminal laws of all civilized nations, and the internal penal laws of the countries in which such crimes were committed'.

Hundreds of thousands of French and Belgian civilians were deported to Germany for use as slave labour, often to work in armaments factories. The indictment continued:

'Such deportees were subjected to the most barbarous conditions of overcrowding; they were provided with wholly insufficient clothing and were given little or no food for several days. The conditions of transport were such that many deportees died in the course of the journey.'

The indictment finally considered in some detail the murder and ill-treatment of hostages and prisoners of war who were 'denied adequate food, shelter, clothing and medical care and attention; by forcing them to labour in inhumane conditions; by torturing them and subjecting them to inhuman indignities and by killing them'.

COUNT FOUR: CRIMES AGAINST HUMANITY

There were two threads to the fourth and final indictment. The first sought to show that the defendants were responsible for the 'murder, extermination, enslavement and other inhumane acts' against civilians both before and during the war. It noted the official adoption of a policy that ensured the 'persecution, repression, and extermination of all civilians in Germany who were, or who were believed to be, or who were believed likely to become, hostile to the Nazi Government ... They imprisoned such persons without judicial process, holding them in "protective custody" and concentration camps, and subjected them to persecution, degradation, despoilment, enslavement, torture, and murder.'

The final part of Count Four was devoted to the genocide of the Jewish population.

'Jews were systematically persecuted since 1933; they were deprived of their liberty, thrown into concentration camps where they were murdered and ill-treated. Their property was confiscated ... Since 1 September 1939, the persecution of the Jews was redoubled: millions of Jews from Germany and from the occupied Western Countries were sent to the Eastern Countries for extermination.'

The majority of the defendants would be tried on one or more of these four counts. The Tribunal would next hear the accusations against the defendants and their pleas.

CHAPTER 3

The Defendants

The afternoon of the first day of the Nuremberg Trials concluded the reading of the indictment. Then followed the appendices to the main document, which were critical in that they contained the reasoning for each of the defendants being placed on trial. All of the defendants were to be charged on the first indictment – participation in a common plan or conspiracy; the three other counts, relating to crimes against peace, war crimes and crimes against humanity, were applied where appropriate.

Sydney S. Alderman of the US prosecution panel began the session by reading Appendix A, which comprised an entry for each defendant.

Hermann Göring
'The Defendant Göring between 1932 and 1945 was a member of the Nazi Party, Supreme Leader of the SA, general in the SS, a member and President of the Reichstag, Minister of the Interior of Prussia, Chief of the Prussian Police and Prussian Secret State Police, Chief of the Prussian State Council, Trustee of the Four Year Plan, Reich Minister for Air, Commander-in-Chief of the Air Force, President of the Council of Ministers for the Defense of the Reich, member of the Secret Cabinet Council, head of the Hermann Göring Industrial Combine, and Successor Designate to Hitler.

'The Defendant Göring used the foregoing positions, his personal influence, and his intimate connection with the Führer in such a manner that: He promoted the accession to power of the Nazi conspirators and the consolidation of their control over Germany set forth in Count One of the Indictment; he promoted the military and economic preparation for war set forth in Count One of the Indictment; he participated in the planning and preparation of the Nazi conspirators for wars of aggression and wars in violation of international treaties, agreements, and assurances set forth in Counts One and Two of the Indictment; and he authorized, directed, and participated in the War Crimes set forth in Count Three of the Indictment, and the Crimes against Humanity set forth in Count Four of the Indictment, including a wide variety of crimes against persons and property.'

Joachim von Ribbentrop

'The Defendant Ribbentrop between 1932 and 1945 was a member of the Nazi Party, a member of the Nazi Reichstag, advisor to the Führer on matters of foreign policy, representative of the Nazi Party for matters of foreign policy, special German delegate for disarmament questions, Ambassador extraordinary, Ambassador in London, organizer and director of Dienststelle Ribbentrop, Reich Minister for Foreign Affairs, member of the Secret Cabinet Council, member of the Führer's political staff at general headquarters, and general in the SS.

'The Defendant Ribbentrop used the foregoing positions, his personal influence, and his intimate connection with the Führer in such a manner that: He promoted the accession to power of the Nazi conspirators as set forth in Count One of the Indictment; he promoted the preparations for war set forth in Count One of the Indictment; he participated in the political planning and preparation of the Nazi conspirators for wars of aggression and wars in violation of international treaties, agreements, and assurances as set forth in Counts One and Two of the Indictment; in accordance with the Fighter Principle he executed and assumed responsibility for the execution of the foreign policy plans of the Nazi conspirators set forth in Count One of the Indictment; and he authorized, directed, and participated in the War Crimes set forth in Count Three of the Indictment and the Crimes against Humanity set forth in Count Four of the Indictment, including more particularly the crimes against persons and property in occupied territories.'

Rudolf Hess

'The Defendant Hess between 1921 and 1941 was a member of the Nazi Party, Deputy to the Führer, Reich Minister without Portfolio, member of the Reichstag, member of the Council of Ministers for the Defense of the Reich, member of the Secret Cabinet Council, Successor Designate to the Führer after the Defendant Göring, a general in the SS and a general in the SA.

'The Defendant Hess used the foregoing positions, his personal influence, and his intimate connection with the Führer in such a manner that: He promoted the accession to power of the Nazi conspirators and the consolidation of their control over Germany set forth in Count One of the Indictment; he promoted the military, economic, and psychological preparations for war set forth in Count One of the Indictment; he participated in the political planning and preparation for wars of aggression and wars in violation of international treaties, agreements, and assurances set forth in Counts One and Two of the Indictment; he participated in the preparation and planning of foreign policy plans of the Nazi conspirators set forth in Count One of the Indictment; he authorized, directed, and participated in the War Crimes set forth in Count Three of the Indictment and the Crimes against Humanity set forth in Count Four of the Indictment, including a wide variety of crimes against persons and property.'

Ernst Kaltenbrunner

'The Defendant Kaltenbrunner between 1932 and 1945 was a member of the Nazi Party, a general in the SS, a member of the

Reichstag, a general of the Police, State Secretary for Security in Austria in charge of the Austrian Police, Police Leader of Vienna, Lower and Upper Austria, Head of the Reich Main Security Office and Chief of the Security Police and Security Service.

'The Defendant Kaltenbrunner used the foregoing positions and his personal influence in such a manner that: He promoted the consolidation of control over Austria seized by the Nazi conspirators as set forth in Count One of the Indictment; and he authorized, directed, and participated in the War Crimes set forth in Count Three of the Indictment and the Crimes against Humanity set forth in Count Four of the Indictment including particularly the Crimes against Humanity involved in the system of concentration camps.'

Alfred Rosenberg

'The Defendant Rosenberg between 1920 and 1940 was a member of the Nazi Party, Nazi member of the Reichstag, Reichsleiter in the Nazi Party for Ideology and Foreign Policy, the editor of the Nazi newspaper *Völkischer Beobachter*, or "People's Observer", and the *NS Monatshefte*, head of the Foreign Political Office of the Nazi Party, Special Delegate for the entire Spiritual and Ideological Training of the Nazi Party, Reich Minister for the Eastern Occupied Territories, organizer of the "Einsatzstab Rosenberg", a general in the SS and a general in the SA.

'The Defendant Rosenberg used the foregoing positions, his personal influence and his intimate connection with the Führer in such a manner that: He developed, disseminated, and exploited the doctrinal techniques of the Nazi conspirators set forth in Count One of the Indictment; he promoted the accession to power of the Nazi conspirators and the consolidation of their control over Germany set forth in Count One of the Indictment; he promoted the psychological preparations for war set forth in Count One of the Indictment; he participated in the political planning and preparation for wars of aggression and wars in violation of international treaties, agreements, and assurances set forth in Counts One and Two of the Indictment; and he authorized, directed, and participated in the War Crimes set forth in Count Three of the Indictment and the Crimes against Humanity set forth in Count Four of the Indictment, including a wide variety of crimes against persons and property."

Hans Frank

'The Defendant Frank between 1932 and 1945 was a member of the Nazi Party, a general in the SS, a member of the Reichstag, Reich Minister without Portfolio, Reich Commissar for the Coordination of Justice, President of the International Chamber of Law and Academy of German Law, Chief of the Civil Administration of Lodz, Supreme Administrative Chief of the military district of West Prussia, Poznan, Lodz, and Krakow, and Governor General of the occupied Polish territories.

'The Defendant Frank used the foregoing positions, his personal influence, and his intimate connection with the Führer in such a manner that: He promoted the accession to power of the Nazi conspirators and the consolidation of their control over Germany set forth in Count One of the Indictment; he authorized, directed, and participated in the War Crimes set forth in Count Three of the Indictment and the Crimes against Humanity set forth in Count Four of the Indictment, including particularly the War Crimes and Crimes against Humanity involved in the administration of occupied territories.'

Martin Bormann

'The Defendant Bormann between 1925 and 1945 was a member of the Nazi Party, member of the Reichstag, a member of the Staff of the Supreme Command of the SA, founder and head of "Hilfskasse der NSDAP", Reichsleiter, Chief of Staff Office of the Führer's Deputy, head of the Party Chancery, Secretary of the Führer, member of the Council of Ministers for the Defense of the Reich, organizer and head of the Volkssturm, a general in the SS, and a general in the SA.

'The Defendant Bormann used the foregoing positions, his personal influence, and his intimate connection with the Führer in such a manner that: He promoted the accession to power of the Nazi conspirators and the consolidation of their control over Germany set forth in Count One of the Indictment; he promoted the preparations for war set forth in Count One of the Indictment; and he authorized, directed, and participated in the War Crimes set forth in Count Three of the Indictment and the Crimes against Humanity set forth in Count Four of the Indictment, including a wide variety of crimes against persons and property.'

Wilhelm Frick

'The Defendant Frick between 1932 and 1945 was a member of the Nazi Party, Reichsleiter, general in the SS, member of the Reichstag, Reich Minister of the Interior, Prussian Minister of the Interior, Reich Director of Elections, General Plenipotentiary for the Administration of the Reich, head of the Central Office for the Reunification of Austria and the German Reich, Director of the Central Office for the Incorporation of Sudetenland, Memel, Danzig, the Eastern Occupied Territories, Eupen, Malmedy, and Moresnet, Director of the Central Office for the Protectorate of Bohemia, Moravia, the Government General, Lower Styria, Upper Carinthia, Norway, Alsace, Lorraine, and all other occupied territories, and Reich Protector for Bohemia and Moravia.

'The Defendant Frick used the foregoing positions, his personal influence, and his intimate connection with the Führer in such a manner that: He promoted the accession to power of the Nazi conspirators and the consolidation of their control over Germany set forth in Count One of the Indictment; he participated in the planning and preparation of the Nazi conspirators for wars of aggression and wars in violation of international treaties, agreements, and assurances set forth in Counts One and Two of the Indictment; and he authorized, directed, and participated in the War Crimes set forth in Count Three of the Indictment and the Crimes against Humanity set forth in Count Four of the Indictment, including more particularly the crimes against persons and property in occupied territories.'

Robert Ley

'The Defendant Ley between 1932 and 1945 was a member of the Nazi Party, Reichsleiter, Nazi Party Organization Manager, member of the Reichstag, leader of the German Labor Front, a general in the SA and Joint Organizer of the Central Inspection for the Care of Foreign Workers.

'The Defendant Ley used the foregoing positions, his personal influence and his intimate connection with the Führer in such a manner that: He promoted the accession to power of the Nazi conspirators and the consolidation of their control over Germany as set forth in Count One of the Indictment; he promoted the preparation for war set forth in Count One of the Indictment; he authorized, directed, and participated in the War Crimes set forth in Count Three of the Indictment, and in the Crimes against Humanity set forth in Count Four of the Indictment, including particularly the War Crimes and Crimes against Humanity relating to the abuse of human beings for labour in the conduct of the aggressive wars.'

Fritz Sauckel

'The Defendant Sauckel between 1921 and 1945 was a member of the Nazi Party, Gauleiter and Reichsstatthalter of Thuringia, a member of the Reichstag, General Plenipotentiary for the Employment of Labor under the Four Year Plan, Joint Organizer with the Defendant Ley of the Central Inspection for the Care of Foreign Workers, a general in the SS, and a general in the SA.

'The Defendant Sauckel used the foregoing positions and his personal influence in such manner that: He promoted the accession to power of the Nazi conspirators set forth in Count One of the Indictment; he participated in the economic preparations for wars of aggression and wars in violation of treaties, agreements, and assurances set forth in Counts One and

Two of the Indictment; he authorized, directed, and participated in the War Crimes set forth in Count Three of the Indictment, and the Crimes against Humanity set forth in Count Four of the Indictment, including particularly the War Crimes and Crimes against Humanity involved in forcing the inhabitants of occupied countries to work as slave laborers in occupied countries and in Germany.'

Albert Speer

'The Defendant Speer between 1932 and 1945 was a member of the Nazi Party, Reichsleiter, member of the Reichstag, Reich Minister for Armament and Munitions, Chief of the Organization Todt, General Plenipotentiary for Armaments in the Office of the Four Year Plan, and Chairman of the Armaments Council.

'The Defendant Speer used the foregoing positions and his personal influence in such a manner that: He participated in the military and economic planning and preparation of the Nazi conspirators for wars of aggression and wars in violation of international treaties, agreements, and assurances set forth in Counts One and Two of the Indictment; and he authorized, directed, and participated in the War Crimes set forth in Count Three of the Indictment and the Crimes against Humanity set forth in Count Four of the Indictment, including more particularly the abuse and exploitation of human beings for forced labor in the conduct of aggressive war.'

Walther Funk

'The Defendant Funk between 1932 and 1945 was a member of the Nazi Party, Economic Adviser of Hitler, National Socialist Deputy to the Reichstag, Press Chief of the Reich Government, State Secretary of the Reich Ministry of Public Enlightenment and Propaganda, Reich Minister of Economics, Prussian Minister of Economics, President of the German Reichsbank, Plenipotentiary for Economy, and member of the Ministerial Council for the Defense of the Reich.

'The Defendant Funk used the foregoing positions, his personal influence, and his close connection with the Führer in such a manner that: He promoted the accession to power of the Nazi conspirators and the consolidation of their control over Germany set forth in Count One of the Indictment; he promoted the preparations for war set forth in Count One of the Indictment; he participated in the military and economic planning and preparation of the Nazi conspirators for wars of aggression and wars in violation of international treaties, agreements, and assurances set forth in Counts One and Two of the Indictment; and he authorized, directed, and participated in the War Crimes set forth in Count Three of the Indictment and the Crimes against Humanity set forth in Count Four of the Indictment, including more particularly crimes against persons and property in connection with the economic exploitation of occupied territories.'

Hjalmar Schacht

'The Defendant Schacht between 1932 and 1945 was a member of the Nazi Party, a member of the Reichstag, Reich Minister of Economics, Reich Minister without Portfolio and President of the German Reichsbank.

'The Defendant Schacht used the foregoing positions, his personal influence, and his connection with the Führer in such a manner that: He promoted the accession to power of the Nazi conspirators and the consolidation of their control over Germany set forth in Count One of the Indictment; he promoted the preparations for war set forth in Count One of the Indictment; and he participated in the military and economic plans and preparation of the Nazi conspirators for wars of aggression, and wars in violation of international treaties, agreements, and assurances set forth in Counts One and Two of the Indictment.'

Franz von Papen

'The Defendant Papen between 1932 and 1945 was a member of the Nazi Party, a member of the Reichstag, Reich Chancellor under Hitler, special Plenipotentiary for the Saar, negotiator of the Concordat with the Vatican, Ambassador in Vienna, and Ambassador in Turkey.

'The Defendant Papen used the foregoing positions, his personal influence, and his close connection with the Führer in such a manner that: He promoted the accession to power of the Nazi conspirators and participated in the consolidation of their control over Germany set forth in Count One of the Indictment; he promoted the preparations for war set forth in Count One of the Indictment and he participated in the political planning and preparation of the Nazi conspirators for wars of aggression and wars in violation of international treaties, agreements, and assurances set forth in Counts One and Two of the Indictment.'

Gustav Krupp von Bohlen und Halbach

'The Defendant Krupp between 1932 and 1945 was head of Friedrich Krupp A.G., a member of the General Economic Council, President of the Reich Union of German Industry, and head of the Group for Mining and Production of Iron and Metals under the Reich Ministry of Economics.

'The Defendant Krupp used the foregoing positions, his personal influence, and his connection with the Führer in such a manner that: He promoted the accession to power of the Nazi conspirators and the consolidation of their control over Germany set forth in Count One of the Indictment; he promoted the preparation for war set forth in Count One of the Indictment; he participated in the military and economic planning and preparation of the Nazi conspirators for wars of aggression and wars in violation of international treaties, agreements, and assurances set forth in Counts One and Two of the Indictment; and he authorized, directed, and participated in the War Crimes set forth in Count Three of the Indictment and the Crimes against Humanity set forth in Count Four of the Indictment, including more particularly the exploitation and abuse of human beings for labour in the conduct of aggressive wars.'

Konstantin von Neurath

'The Defendant Neurath between 1932 and 1945 was a member of the Nazi Party, a general in the SS, a member of the Reichstag, Reich Minister, Reich Minister of Foreign Affairs, President of the Secret Cabinet Council, and Reich Protector for Bohemia and Moravia.

'The Defendant Neurath used the foregoing positions, his personal influence, and his close connection with the Führer in such a manner that: He promoted the accession to power of the Nazi conspirators set forth in Count One of the Indictment; he promoted the preparations for war set forth in Count One of the Indictment; he participated in the political planning and preparation of the Nazi conspirators for wars of aggression and wars in violation of international treaties, agreements, and assurances set forth in Counts One and Two of the Indictment; in accordance with the Führer Principle he executed, and assumed responsibility for, the execution of the foreign policy plans of the Nazi conspirators set forth in Count One of the Indictment; and he authorized, directed, and participated in the War Crimes set forth in Count Three of the Indictment and the Crimes against Humanity set forth in Count Four of the Indictment, including particularly the crimes against persons and property in the occupied territories.'

Baldur Benedikt von Schirach

'The Defendant Schirach between 1924 and 1945 was a member of the Nazi Party, a member of the Reichstag, Reich Youth Leader on the Staff of the SA Supreme Command, Reichsleiter in the Nazi Party for Youth Education, Leader of Youth of the German Reich, head of the Hitler Jugend, Reich Defense Commissioner, and Reichsstatthalter and Gauleiter of Vienna.

'The Defendant Schirach used the foregoing positions, his personal influence, and his intimate connection with the Führer in such a manner that: He promoted the accession to power of the Nazi conspirators and the consolidation of their control over Germany set forth in Count One of the Indictment; he promoted the psychological and educational preparations for war and the militarization of Nazi-dominated organizations set forth in Count One of the Indictment; and he authorized, directed, and participated in the Crimes against Humanity set forth in Count Four of the Indictment, including, particularly, anti-Jewish measures.'

Arthur Seyss-Inquart

'The Defendant Seyss-Inquart between 1932 and 1945 was a member of the Nazi Party, a general in the SS, State Councillor of Austria, Minister of the Interior and Security of Austria, Chancellor of Austria, a member of the Reichstag, a member of the Reich Cabinet, Reich Minister without Portfolio, Chief of the Civil Administration in South Poland, Deputy Governor General of the Polish occupied territory, and Reich Commissar for the occupied Netherlands. The Defendant Seyss-Inquart used the foregoing positions and his personal influence in such a manner that: He promoted the seizure and the consolidation of control over Austria by the Nazi conspirators set forth in Count One of the Indictment; he participated in the political planning and preparation of the Nazi conspirators for wars of aggression and wars in violation of international treaties, agreements, and assurances set forth in Counts One and Two of the Indictment; and he authorized, directed, and participated in the War Crimes set forth in Count Three of the Indictment and the Crimes against Humanity set forth in Count Four of the Indictment, including a wide variety of crimes against persons and property.'

Julius Streicher

'The Defendant Streicher between 1932 and 1945 was a member of the Nazi Party, a member of the Reichstag, a general in the SA, Gauleiter of Franconia, and editor-in-chief of the anti-Semitic newspaper *Der Stürmer*.

'The Defendant Streicher used the foregoing positions, his

personal influence, and his close connection with the Führer in such a manner that: He promoted the accession to power of the Nazi conspirators and the consolidation of their control over Germany set forth in Count One of the Indictment; he authorized, directed, and participated in the Crimes against Humanity set forth in Count Four of the Indictment, including particularly the incitement of the persecution of the Jews set forth in Count One and Count Four of the Indictment.'

Wilhelm Keitel

'The Defendant Keitel between 1938 and 1945 was Chief of the High Command of the German Armed Forces, member of the Secret Cabinet Council, member of the Council of Ministers for the Defense of the Reich, and Field Marshal.

'The Defendant Keitel used the foregoing positions, his personal influence, and his intimate connection with the Führer in such a manner that: He promoted the military preparations for war set forth in Count One of the Indictment; he participated in the political planning and preparation of the Nazi conspirators for wars of aggression and wars in violation of international treaties, agreements, and assurances set forth in Counts One and Two of the Indictment; he executed and assumed responsibility for the execution of the plans of the Nazi conspirators for wars of aggression and wars in violation of international treaties, agreements, and assurances set forth in Counts One and Two of the Indictment; he authorized, directed, and participated in the War Crimes set forth in Count Three of the Indictment and the Crimes against Humanity set forth in Count Four of the Indictment, including particularly the War Crimes and Crimes against Humanity involved in the ill-treatment of prisoners of war and of the civilian population of occupied territories.'

Alfred Jodl

'The Defendant Jodl between 1932 and 1945 was Lieutenant Colonel, Army Operations Department of the Wehrmacht,

Colonel, Chief of OKW Operations Department, Major General and Chief of Staff OKW and Colonel General.

'The Defendant Jodl used the foregoing positions, his personal influence, and his close connection with the Führer in such a manner that: He promoted the accession to power of the Nazi conspirators and the consolidation of their control over Germany set forth in Count One of the Indictment; he promoted the preparations for war set forth in Count One of the Indictment; he participated in the military planning and preparation of the Nazi conspirators for wars of aggression and wars in violation of international treaties, agreements, and assurances set forth in Counts One and Two of the Indictment; and he authorized, directed, and participated in the War Crimes set forth in Count Three of the Indictment and the Crimes against Humanity set forth in Count Four of the Indictment, including a wide variety of crimes against persons and property.'

Erich Raeder

'The Defendant Raeder between 1928 and 1945 was Commander-in-Chief of the German Navy, Generaladmiral, Grossadmiral, Admiralinspekteur of the German Navy, and a member of the Secret Cabinet Council.

'The Defendant Raeder used the foregoing positions and his personal influence in such a manner that: He promoted the preparations for war set forth in Count One of the Indictment; he participated in the political planning and preparation of the Nazi conspirators for wars of aggression and wars in violation of international treaties, agreements, and assurances set forth in Counts One and Two of the Indictment; he executed, and assumed responsibility for the execution of the plans of the Nazi conspirators for wars of aggression and wars in violation of international treaties, agreements, and assurances set forth in Counts One and Two of the Indictment; and he authorized, directed, and participated in the War Crimes set forth in Count

Three of the Indictment, including particularly War Crimes arising out of sea warfare.'

Karl Dönitz

'The Defendant Dönitz between 1932 and 1945 was Commanding Officer of the Weddigen U-boat Flotilla, Commander-in-Chief of the U-boat arm, Vice-Admiral, Admiral, Grossadmiral, and Commander-in-Chief of the German Navy, advisor to Hitler, and successor to Hitler as head of the German Government.

'The Defendant Dönitz used the foregoing positions, his personal influence, and his intimate connection with the Führer in such a manner that: He promoted the preparations for war set forth in Count One of the Indictment; he participated in the military planning and preparation of the Nazi conspirators for wars of aggression and wars in violation of international treaties, agreements, and assurances set forth in Counts One and Two of the Indictment; and he authorized, directed, and participated in the War Crimes set forth in Count Three of the Indictment, including particularly the crimes against persons and property on the High Seas.'

Hans Fritzsche

'The Defendant Fritzsche between 1933 and 1945 was a member of the Nazi Party, editor-in-chief of the official German news agency, "Deutsches Nachrichten Buro", head of the Wireless News Service and of the Home Press Division of the Reich Ministry of Propaganda, Ministerialdirektor of the Reich Ministry of Propaganda, Head of the Radio Division of the Propaganda Department of the Nazi Party, and Plenipotentiary for the Political Organization of the Greater German Radio.

'The Defendant Fritzsche used the foregoing positions and his personal influence to disseminate and exploit the principal doctrines of the Nazi conspirators set forth in Count One of the Indictment, and to advocate, encourage, and incite the commission of the War Crimes set forth in Count Three of the Indictment and the Crimes against Humanity set forth in Count Four of the Indictment including, particularly, anti-Jewish measures and the ruthless exploitation of occupied territories.'

During the reading of the charges, the focus of the press and other onlookers in the gallery of Courtroom 600 was firmly on the defendants themselves. The pompous Göring clearly considered himself the star of the show and reacted throughout the proceedings with exaggerated nodding of the head and facial gestures. He wanted the whole room to be left in no doubt as to what he felt about the indictments. At lunchtime the courtroom was cleared but the defendants were ordered to remain in place while they were fed; they were heard to joke about the sudden improved quality of the food on offer now they were on display to the world. At around 4 p.m., Ribbentrop collapsed and had to be removed by guards. He was given a sedative pill and returned 20 minutes later. At several points during the afternoon, Nazi economist Funk – outraged that he was even on trial – appeared on the verge of losing his temper, but most others in the dock, the press reported, carried themselves with a sense of self-righteous disdain or defiance.

Following the reading of the individual charges, Alderman proceeded with Appendix B of the indictment, which laid out the charges against groups and organizations: the Reich Cabinet, specific groups within the Nazi Party, the SS, the SA, the Gestapo and the High Command of the German Armed Forces.

The day was concluded by Sir David Maxwell Fyfe of the British prosecution, who read out the final part of the indictment, covering violations of international agreements in the course of 'planning, preparing and initiating the wars'. This was an extremely detailed list of 26 separate charges covering every German violation of treaty and agreement, from the first Hague Conference in July 1899 to the declaration of war with the United States in December 1941.

The pleas

Day two of the Nuremberg Trials, Wednesday, 21 November 1945, would see the defendants being involved for the first time. They were called by the President of the Tribunal, Sir Geoffrey Lawrence, to give their pleas. The day began with requests from members of the defence counsel. Dr Ralph Thoma, who represented defendant Alfred Rosenberg, claimed that he had not been given the opportunity to discuss the plea with his client, nor had other members of the defence. An irritated Lawrence responded: 'I would point out to the defendants' counsel that they have had several weeks' preparation for this trial … But now we will adjourn for 15 minutes in which all of you may consult with your clients.'

Before the courtroom adjourned, Thoma raised a further procedural question by enquiring whether the defendants would have to enter a single-word plea or 'whether a more extensive and longer statement could be made'.

Lawrence responded by citing Article 24 of the Charter: '"The Tribunal shall ask each defendant whether he pleads guilty or not guilty." That is what they have got to do at that stage. Of course, the defendants will have a full opportunity themselves, if they are called as witnesses, and by their counsel, to make their defence fully at a later stage.'

Following the recess, Lawrence asked each of the defendants to enter their plea, beginning with Hermann Göring, the highest-ranking Nazi on trial. Clearly with a lengthier statement in mind, Göring began: 'Before I answer the question of the Tribunal whether or not I am guilty … ' But before he could go any further, Lawrence interjected: 'I informed the Court that defendants were not entitled to make a statement. You must plead guilty or not guilty.'

[Hermann Göring] 'I declare myself in the sense of the Indictment not guilty.'

[Rudolf Hess] 'No!'

'That will be entered as a plea of not guilty,' Lawrence interjected, to laughter around the room. 'If there is any disturbance in court, those who make it will have to leave the court,' he remarked curtly.

[Joachim von Ribbentrop] 'I declare myself in the sense of the Indictment not guilty.'

[Wilhelm Keitel] 'I declare myself not guilty.'

Ernst Kaltenbrunner, the highest-ranking member of the SS to face trial at Nuremberg, was incapacitated through a subarachnoid haemorrhage and remained in the nearby military hospital. Lawrence declared that the trial would proceed without him and that he would be given the opportunity to enter his plea when he was well enough to return to court.

[Alfred Rosenberg] 'I declare myself in the sense of the Indictment not guilty.'

[Hans Frank] 'I declare myself not guilty.'

[Wilhelm Frick] 'Not guilty.'

[Julius Streicher] 'Not guilty.'

[Walther Funk] 'I declare myself not guilty.'

[Hjalmar Schacht] 'I am not guilty in any respect.'

[Karl Dönitz] 'Not guilty.'

[Erich Raeder] 'I declare myself not guilty.'

[Baldur von Schirach] 'I declare myself in the sense of the Indictment not guilty.'

[Fritz Sauckel] 'I declare myself in the sense of the Indictment, before God and the world and particularly before my people, not guilty.'

[Alfred Jodl] 'Not guilty. For what I have done or had to do, I have a pure conscience before God, before history and my people.'

[Franz von Papen] 'I declare myself in no way guilty.'

[Arthur Seyss-Inquart] 'I declare myself not guilty.'

[Albert Speer] 'Not guilty.'

[Konstantin von Neurath] 'I answer the question in the negative.'

[Hans Fritzsche] 'As regards this Indictment, not guilty.'

At this point, Hermann Göring again stood up in the prisoners' dock and attempted to address the room but once more he was told that he had no entitlement to address the Tribunal except through his counsel. He sat down indignantly.

The United States chief prosecutor Justice Robert Jackson then rose to the lectern. His epic opening address would take up the rest of the second day of the Tribunal.

CHAPTER 4

The Opening Addresses

Responsibility for proving the four indictments to the court was split among the four Allied prosecution teams. Since it fell to the Americans to outline the conspiracy charge – Count One – the opening address was to be given by the US chief prosecutor, Robert Houghwout Jackson. Born in Pennsylvania and raised in New York, in spite of his modest education and lack of a university degree Jackson had risen from apprenticeship in a legal practice to the lofty peak of Associate Supreme Court of Justice, and had been President Truman's first choice to take on the role of America's lead prosecutor at Nuremberg. A fast talker by nature, during pre-trial sessions he had been asked to slow down on more than one occasion – or even stop – by interpreters who struggled with simultaneous translations at his natural speed; as a reminder, when he stood at the lectern to open the case for the prosecution the front page of his notes was marked with the word 'slowly'. His address would take the remainder of the day. Almost six months in preparation, with numerous revisions, Jackson's opening statement is still regarded by many as one of the great pieces of oratory.

'The privilege of opening the first trial in history for crimes against the peace of the world imposes a grave responsibility. The wrongs which we seek to condemn and punish have been so calculated, so malignant, and so devastating, that civilization cannot tolerate their being ignored, because it cannot survive their being repeated.

US chief prosecutor, Robert Houghwout Jackson.

'That four great nations, flushed with victory and stung with injury, stay the hand of vengeance and voluntarily submit their captive enemies to the judgment of the law is one of the most significant tributes that power has ever paid to reason ... This inquest represents the practical effort of four of the most mighty of nations, with the support of 15 more, to utilize international law to meet the greatest menace of our times – aggressive war.'

It was a powerful way of setting the scene for the prosecution. Jackson, in particular, had argued the case for a punishment based on law rather than the summary revenge that his Soviet counterparts had seemed to prefer. He also approached the thorny issue of 'victors' justice':

'Unfortunately, the nature of these crimes is such that both prosecution and judgment must be by victor nations over vanquished foes. The worldwide scope of the aggressions carried out by these men has left but few real neutrals. Either the victors must judge the vanquished or we must leave the defeated to judge themselves. After the First World War, we learned the futility of the latter course.'

Here he was referring to the farcical trials held in Germany after the First World War that saw only half a dozen prosecutions, followed by minimal jail sentences. This could not be allowed to happen again.

Jackson was under no illusion about the problematic issues facing the International Military Tribunal. Yet although he conceded that the Tribunal was 'novel and experimental' he was nonetheless certain that the crimes covered in the indictments were well established in international law.

He then turned his attention to the defendants themselves, the '20-odd broken men', as he described them.

'... Merely as individuals their fate is of little consequence to the world. What makes this inquest significant is that these prisoners represent sinister influences that will lurk in the world long after their bodies have returned to dust. We will show them to be living symbols of racial hatreds, of terrorism and violence, and of the arrogance and cruelty of power. They are symbols of fierce nationalisms and of militarism, of intrigue and war-making which have embroiled Europe generation after generation, crushing its manhood, destroying its homes, and impoverishing its life. They have so identified themselves with the philosophies they conceived and with the forces they directed that any tenderness to them is a victory and an encouragement to all the evils which are attached to their names ... We will give you undeniable proofs of incredible events. The catalog of crimes will omit nothing that could be conceived by a pathological pride, cruelty, and lust for power.'

The American case was centred on the belief that the behaviour of the accused could not be considered 'conduct that is ... natural and human ... It is not because they yielded to the normal frailties of human beings that we accuse them. It is their abnormal and inhuman conduct which brings them to this bar.'

The prosecution statement made a significant early point, clarifying that this process should not be seen as the people of Germany facing trial:

'We have no purpose to incriminate the whole German people. We know that the Nazi Party was not put in power by a majority of the German vote. We know it came to power by an evil alliance between the most extreme of the Nazi revolutionists, the most unrestrained of the German reactionaries, and the most aggressive of the German militarists ... The German people should know by now that the people of the United States hold them in no fear and in no hate ... The case as presented by the United States will be concerned with the brains and authority back of all the crimes. These defendants were men of a station and rank which does not soil its own hands with blood. They were men who knew how to use lesser folk as tools. We want to reach the planners and designers, the inciters and leaders without whose evil architecture the world would not have been for so long scourged with the violence and lawlessness, and wracked with the agonies and convulsions, of this terrible war.'

The core of Jackson's introduction and the American case was to prove the premeditated nature of the Nazi atrocities from the earliest days of the organization's existence.

'This war did not just happen. It was planned and prepared for over a long period of time and with no small skill and cunning. The world has perhaps never seen such a concentration and stimulation of the energies of any people as that which enabled Germany 20 years after it was defeated, disarmed, and dismembered to come so near carrying out its plan to dominate Europe. Whatever else we may say of those who were the authors of this war, they did achieve a stupendous work in organization, and our first task is to examine the means by which these defendants and their fellow conspirators prepared and incited Germany to go to war.

'In general, our case will disclose these defendants all uniting at some time with the Nazi Party in a plan which they well knew could be accomplished only by an outbreak of war in Europe. Their seizure of the German State, their subjugation of the German people, their terrorism and extermination of dissident elements, their planning and waging of war, their calculated and planned ruthlessness in the conduct of warfare, their deliberate and planned criminality toward conquered peoples – all these are ends for which they acted in concert.'

Jackson went on at length to outline the aims of Hitler and the Nazi Party and how it went about achieving them. In a segment of his speech he referred to as 'The Lawless Road to Power', he conceded that the Party: 'made a strong appeal to that sort of nationalism which in ourselves we call patriotism and in our rivals chauvinism', and that: 'Some of its purposes would commend themselves to many good citizens, such as the demands for profit-sharing in the great industries, generous development of provision for old age, creation and maintenance of a healthy middle class ... and raising the standard of health.'

Moving on to Germany's territorial ambitions, Jackson asserted the fundamental legitimacy of some aspects of Nazi foreign policy, particularly the overall aim of achieving a Greater Germany through the pursuit of '*Lebensraum*' ('land and territory – colonies – for the enrichment of our people and the settlement of our surplus population'), but only 'if they were to be attained without resort to aggressive warfare'. Yet it was clear from the Party's inception, he suggested, that not only was aggressive war always under contemplation but also: 'The Party program foreshadowed the campaign of terrorism. It announced, "We demand ruthless war upon those whose activities are injurious to the common interests", and it demanded that such offenses be punished with death.'

Jackson began to describe how the Nazi Party went about consolidating power by quoting the words of Colonel General Werner von Fritsch in 1938:

'Shortly after the first war I came to the conclusion that we should have to be victorious in three battles if Germany were to become powerful again: The battle against the working class ... Against the Catholic Church ... Against the Jews.'

These were battles that Hitler had to win if he was to consolidate power once he had become Chancellor in 1933. Jackson began with the trade unions, and the role of Robert Ley in subsuming Germany's four-and-a-half million trade unionists into the Deutsche Arbeitsfront (German Labour Front) by effectively banning trade unions and seizing their assets.

'Not only did the Nazis dominate and regiment German labor, but they forced the youth into the ranks of the laboring people they had thus led into chains.'

He ended with a scathing personal assessment: 'Robert Ley, the field marshal of the battle against labour, answered our Indictment with suicide. Apparently he knew no better answer.'

Of the question of the Church, Jackson quoted a secret decree from Martin Bormann issued in June 1941:

> 'Only the Reich Government and by its direction the Party, its components, and attached units have a right to leadership of the people ... so must the possibility of church influence also be totally removed ... Not until then are people and Reich secure in their existence for all the future.'

Jackson then read from Gestapo transcripts of how violent demonstrations against the Roman Catholic Church had been organized by the Party. Unsurprisingly, the most harrowing claims came in relation to the Nazi treatment of German Jews.

> 'The most savage and numerous crimes planned and committed by the Nazis were those against the Jews ... It is my purpose to show a plan and design, to which all Nazis were fanatically committed, to annihilate all Jewish people ... The persecution of the Jews was a continuous and deliberate policy. It was a policy directed against other nations as well as against the Jews themselves. Anti-Semitism was promoted to divide and embitter the democratic peoples and to soften their resistance to the Nazi aggression.'

Again, Jackson turned to the now-deceased Robert Ley for clear evidence of the ultimate Nazi policy. He quoted from the 14 May 1944 edition of the Berlin Nazi newspaper *Der Angriff* (The Attack): 'The second German secret weapon is Anti-Semitism because if it is constantly pursued by Germany, it will become a universal problem which all nations will be forced to consider.'

Jackson further described the Nazi anti-Semitism process as a 'spearhead of terror', quoting the words of defendant Julius Streicher in his newspaper *Der Stürmer*:

'It is also not only a European problem! The Jewish question is a world question! Not only is Germany not safe in the face of the Jews as long as one Jew lives in Europe, but also the Jewish question is hardly solved in Europe so long as Jews live in the rest of the world.'

Much of Jackson's opening statement emphasized the point that the evidence against the Nazis was predominantly self-incriminating.

'The eastern Jew has suffered as no people ever suffered. Their sufferings were carefully reported to the Nazi authorities to show faithful adherence to the Nazi design. I shall refer only to enough of the evidence of these to show the extent of the Nazi design for killing Jews. If I should recite these horrors in words of my own, you would think me intemperate and unreliable. Fortunately, we need not take the word of any witness but the Germans themselves.'

He went on to list examples taken directly from Nazi field reports in the Baltic states and the East from as early as 1941:

'The sum total of the Jews liquidated in Lithuania amounts to 71,105 ... In Latvia, up to now a total of 30,000 Jews were executed ... In Vitebsk 3,000 Jews were liquidated because of the danger of epidemics ... In Kiev 33,771 Jews were executed on September 29 and 30 in retaliation for some fires which were set off there.'

Again, Jackson referred to Nazi documents that described 'the depths of degradation to which the tormentors stooped'. He referred to a report made to the defendant Alfred Rosenberg:

'In the presence of an SS man, a Jewish dentist has to break all gold teeth and fillings out of the mouth of German and Russian

Jews before they are executed ... Men, women and children are locked into barns and burned alive ... Peasants, women and children are shot on the pretext that they are suspected of belonging to bands.'

Here Jackson makes his first reference to the use of gas in the extermination of captives.

'We of the Western World heard of gas wagons in which Jews and political opponents were asphyxiated. We could not believe it.'

He gave examples from reports of the horrific use of mobile gas vans: 'Vehicles well-known to authorities and the civilian population which calls them "death vans".'

The purpose of ridding Germany of its Jews, its trade unions and the influence of the Church, he said, was that the Nazis saw them as:

'obstruction to the precipitation of aggressive war ... Terrorism was the chief instrument for securing the cohesion of the German people in war purposes. Moreover, these cruelties in Germany served as atrocity practice to discipline the membership of the criminal organization to follow the pattern later in occupied countries.'

As the afternoon wore on, Jackson continued with a seemingly endless selection of evidence of Nazi crimes taken directly from their own documents. Under a heading of 'Terrorism and Preparation for War', he highlighted how SS leader Heinrich Himmler had given permission to carry out experiments at the Dachau concentration camp. Germany, he said, 'became one vast torture chamber'.

Under 'Experiments in Aggression' Jackson illustrated how before launching into a full-scale aggressive war – that would begin with the invasion of Poland – the Germans undertook 'cautious experiments to test the spirit of resistance of those who lay across their path'. Thus the Nazi reoccupation of the Rhineland and the annexation of Austria and the Sudetenland region of Czechoslovakia could be seen as testing the water, to assess the reaction of the international community.

Under Jackson's category of 'War of Aggression', extracts from German High Command documents, including the diaries of General Alfred Jodl, provided damning evidence, he claimed, that plans for waging war 'had been laid long in advance'. Indeed, he continued,

'as early as 1935 Hitler appointed the Defendant Schacht to the position of General Deputy for the War Economy ... Not the least incriminating are the minutes of Hitler's meeting with his high advisers. As early as November 5, 1937 Hitler told Defendants Göring, Raeder, and Neurath, among others, that German rearmament was practically accomplished and that he had decided to secure by force, starting with a lightning attack on Czechoslovakia and Austria, greater living space for Germans in Europe no later than 1943–45 and perhaps as early as 1938.'

Jackson next turned to 'Crimes in the Conduct of War', in which he argued that as regrettable as the act of war may be, international conventions had existed to which Germany had been a signatory.

'Even the most warlike of peoples have recognized in the name of humanity some limitations on the savagery of warfare ... The enemy was entitled to surrender and to receive quarter and good treatment as a prisoner of war. We will show by German documents that these rights were denied, that prisoners of war were given brutal treatment and often murdered.'

He cited a top secret order from Hitler, dated 18 October 1942, 'that Commandos, regardless of condition, were "to be slaughtered to the last man" after capture'. He described the policy of deportation from occupied territory as 'Perhaps the deportation to slave labour was the most horrible and extensive slaving operation in history', and cited a speech made in 1944 by defendant Hans Frank, Governor General of Poland, who had boasted: 'I have sent 1,300,000 Polish workers into the Reich.'

The most significant parts of the remainder of the opening statement focused on legal aspects of the prosecution case, in particular the extent to which individuals are responsible for their participation in war crimes or the incitement of others to commit them.

'The idea that a state – any more than a corporation – commits crimes is a fiction. Crimes always are committed only by persons … one who has committed criminal acts may not take refuge in superior orders nor in the doctrine that his crimes were acts of states … No defense based on either of these doctrines can be entertained. Modern civilization puts unlimited weapons of destruction in the hands of men. It cannot tolerate so vast an area of legal irresponsibility.'

The Tribunal, however, was compelled to consider the circumstances, implying 'common sense limits to liability'.

Jackson used the example of a conscripted private taking part in a firing squad as having no power to prevent it taking place. But he was quick to remind the court of the actions of the defendants:

'None of these men before you acted in minor parts. Each of them was entrusted with broad discretion and exercised great power. Their responsibility is correspondingly great and may not be shifted to that fictional being, The State, which cannot be produced for trial, cannot testify, and cannot be sentenced.'

Robert Jackson concluded his opening with what he saw to be the responsibility of the Tribunal. The desire for revenge among the Allies was understandable, but he made the point that the United States was

'… perhaps in a position to be the most dispassionate, for, having sustained the least injury, it is perhaps the least animated by vengeance. Our American cities have not been bombed by day and by night … Our countrymen have not had their homes destroyed over their heads. The menace of Nazi aggression, except to those in actual service, has seemed less personal and immediate to us than to European peoples.'

But he stressed that the United States was no less determined to see justice served.

Jackson's final words were poignant, that it was civilization itself that was the 'real complaining party'.

'Civilization asks whether law is so laggard as to be utterly helpless to deal with crimes of this magnitude by criminals of this order of importance. It does not expect that you can make war impossible. It does expect that your juridical action will put the forces of international law, its precepts, its prohibitions and, most of all, its sanctions, on the side of peace, so that men and women of good will, in all countries, may have leave to live by no man's leave, underneath the law.'

Robert H. Jackson's opening was given wide coverage in the world's press. Most were horrified by the graphic nature of the evidence; for many members of the public this was the first time that specific Nazi atrocities had been reported in such detail. But this was just the beginning.

CHAPTER 5

Presenting the Evidence

After Robert Jackson's courtroom tour de force, little of interest passed over the days that immediately followed. The events of 22 November kicked off with reports relating to two of the defendants. Before the trial began, Julius Streicher's defence counsel had filed an application that he should undergo a medical examination, believing him to be mentally unfit to face the court. Yet having been assessed by three medical experts he was declared sane. At the same time, Martin Bormann's counsel attempted to have his trial postponed, since nobody knew for certain if he was alive or dead. Again, the court refused to compromise: he would be tried *in absentia*, as planned. What followed was a continuation of the prosecution's conspiracy case, delivered mainly by Colonel Robert Storey, one of Robert Jackson's assistants. The press and gallery were visibly bored as one incriminating document followed another, punctuated only by a dispute about an insufficient number of duplicated copies.

Monday, 26 November – the fifth day of the trial – saw the presentation by Sidney Alderman of the United States' case regarding the conspiracy to wage aggressive war. In among the plethora of charts depicting the Nazi advances made at the outset of the war came important documentary evidence of Hitler's intentions. The so-called Hossbach Memorandum gave a detailed summary of a meeting that took place on 5 November 1937 between the Führer and the heads of his military – includlng defendants Göring, Raeder and Neurath – in which his expansionist foreign policies were outlined. Military gains as far ahead as 1945 were contemplated. It was, Alderman declared: 'One of the most striking and revealing of all the captured documents which have come to hand.'

This was followed by the minutes of a conference between Hitler and 14 of his military leaders on 23 May 1939, in which Poland – 'always on the side of our adversaries' – and England were identified as enemies.

> 'The Führer doubts the possibility of a peaceful settlement with England. We must prepare ourselves for the conflict ... England is therefore our enemy, and the conflict with England will be a life-and-death struggle.'

Finally, Alderman presented an address given by Hitler to three of his commanders at Obersalzberg on 22 August 1939, a week before the invasion of Poland:

> 'It was clear to me that a conflict with Poland had to come sooner or later. I had already made this decision in the spring. But I thought I would first turn against the West in a few years, and only afterwards against the East ... I wanted to establish an acceptable relationship with Poland, in order to fight first against the West, but this plan, which was agreeable to me, could not be executed ... I am only afraid that at the last minute some "*Schweinehund*" will make a proposal for mediation.'

The defence immediately cast doubts on the veracity of the Hossbach notes, but the other documents made Hitler's intentions unequivocal. He was intent on waging war:

> 'I shall give a propagandistic cause for starting the war, never mind whether it be plausible or not. The victor shall not be asked, later on, whether we told the truth or not. In starting and making a war, not the right is what matters, but victory. Have no pity. Brutal attitude. Eighty million people shall get what is

their right. Their existence has to be secured. The strongest has the right.'

The new evidence was both damning and shocking, even to some of the defendants. The *New York Herald Tribune* even went as far as publishing the evidence in full. Once again, the public in the West were given new insights into the Nazi regime. But worse was to come.

Cinematic evidence

Sidney Alderman completed the presentation of his documentary evidence mid-afternoon on 29 November and requested that a film be played on the courtroom projector. He handed over to his colleague, prosecutor Thomas Dodd:

> 'The Prosecution for the United States will at this time present to the Tribunal, with its permission, a documentary film on concentration camps. This is by no means the entire proof which the prosecution will offer with respect to the subject of concentration camps, but this film which we offer represents in a brief and unforgettable form an explanation of what the words "concentration camp" imply … We propose to show that concentration camps were not an end in themselves but rather they were an integral part of the Nazi system of government.
>
> '… We intend to prove that each and every one of these defendants knew of the existence of these concentration camps; that fear and terror and nameless horror of the concentration camps were instruments by which the defendants retained power and suppressed opposition of their policies, including, of course, their plans for aggressive war.'

Stories of the concentration camps had created a sensational reaction when they first appeared in British and American newspapers several months prior to the trial. Yet the use of film as a means of capturing what amounted to a crime scene was unprecedented. The film, prosaically titled *Nazi Concentration Camps*, had been compiled from footage shot by military photographers as the Allies liberated the areas in which the camps had been located.

Nobody in Courtroom 600 would forget what they were about to see. Filmed at the Leipzig, Hadamar, Buchenwald, Mauthausen, Dachau and Belsen concentration camps, scene after scene depicted endless piles of gaunt, lifeless bodies, some burned to a crisp. In some cases the corpses were stacked up so high that a bulldozer had to be used to push them into mass graves. Another, filmed at Nordhausen after it had been liberated by the American 3rd Armored and 104th Infantry divisions, showed 2,500 bodies stacked up alongside a bombed-out building. And among the gruesome relics on display were lampshades, picture frames and bookmarks made from the skin of the Nazis' victims.

When the 52-minute documentary ended those present in the courtroom sat in stunned silence. Some in the public gallery wept openly. Many of the defendants, too, were unable to bear these shocking scenes. Prison psychologist Gilbert observed them while the film was showing and made notes on each one:

> 'Funk covers his eyes ... Sauckel mops brow ... Frank swallows hard, blinks eyes, trying to stifle tears ... Frank mutters "Horrible!" ... Rosenberg fidgets, peeks at screen, bows head, looks to see how others are reacting ... Seyss-Inquart stoic throughout ... Speer looks very sad, swallows hard ... Defense attorneys are now muttering, "for God's sake – terrible." ... Fritzsche, pale, biting lips, really seems in agony ... Dönitz has head buried in his hands ... Keitel now hanging head.'

It truly brought the horrors of the Holocaust into the courtroom more powerfully than the dry readings of any number of official documents.

The testimony of Erwin von Lahousen

The first witness to be called in the Nuremberg Trials was Austrian intelligence officer Erwin von Lahousen. As assistant to Admiral Wilhelm Canaris, chief of the Abwehr (Germany's military intelligence), who had turned against the Führer, Lahousen had recorded numerous meetings with Hitler, Keitel and other high-ranking Nazis. Lahousen's testimony would deeply implicate Keitel and Ribbentrop in particular. He described plots to assassinate French generals Giraud and Weygand and plans to provoke an uprising in Eastern Europe, in order to provide an excuse for the slaughter of peasants and Jews. The defendants were visibly shocked by the presence of Lahousen, especially when he spoke of the efforts of his superior, Canaris, to sabotage orders from above and plot against Hitler. The outraged Göring branded him 'a traitor'.

Lahousen's presence had also been a surprise to the defence counsel, who were caught off-guard and struggled to mount an effective cross-examination.

The British case

The breadth of the American approach posed difficulties and annoyances for the three other Allied prosecution teams. Nominally responsible for the conspiracy charges, the Americans had bombarded the court with documentary evidence that covered the other three indictments, a good deal of which had been supplied by the other countries' representatives. Sir David Maxwell Fyfe had earlier attempted to define clear areas of responsibility but America's lead prosecutor, Robert Jackson, showed little interest in compromise, arguing that any document relevant to the conspiracy charge could be used legitimately by the American team.

The morning session of 4 December 1945 saw the commencement of the British prosecution case. Led by Sir Hartley Shawcross, the British case on crimes against peace was interleaved with the American prosecution submission on conspiracy to wage aggressive war. With his dry dispassionate delivery, Shawcross could hardly have been more different in approach to Robert Jackson. Indeed, reporting on the trial, the *Daily Express* newspaper likened his manner to an academic giving a lecture to a 'learned society'.

Shawcross began with a quotation from none other than Adolf Hitler: 'The victor shall not be asked later on whether he told the truth or not. In starting and making a war, not the right is what matters, but victory – the strongest has the right.'

He countered with what he saw as the Allied rationale for the Tribunal:

The British Prosecuting Counsel at the Nuremberg Trials in Germany. From left to right (back row) Major J. Harcourt Barrington, Major Elwyn Jones, E.G. Robey, Lieutenant Colonel J.M.G. Griffith Jones, Colonel H.J. Phillimore; (front row) Sir David Maxwell Fyfe, Sir Hartley Shawcross and G.D. Roberts.

'We realize that victory is not enough, that might is not necessarily right, that lasting peace and the rule of international law is not to be secured by the strong arm alone.'

Shawcross saw the second indictment as a task of two parts:

> 'The first is to demonstrate the nature and the basis of the Crime against Peace ... by waging wars of aggression and in violation of treaties; and the second is to establish beyond all possibility of doubt that such wars were waged by these defendants.'

He was, however, clear in the view that Nazi Germany's waging of a war of aggression was not a criminal act because the victors claimed it to be so ('Vae Victis! Let them pay the penalty of defeat') but because it was already a part of international law.

> 'There must be acknowledged not only, as in the Charter of the United Nations, fundamental human rights, but also, as in the Charter of this Tribunal [Charter of London], fundamental human duties ... none is more fundamental than the duty not to vex the peace of nations in violation of the clearest legal prohibitions and undertakings. If this be an innovation, it is an innovation which we are prepared to defend and to justify, but it is not an innovation which creates a new crime. International law had already, before the Charter was adopted, constituted aggressive war a criminal act.'

There had been, by his calculation, 99 international agreements relating to the indictment – to most of which Germany had been a signatory.

Shawcross then moved on to the personal answerability of the defendants, making it clear that they could not expect to hide behind the notion of national responsibility:

> 'The state is not an abstract entity. Its rights and duties are the rights and duties of men. Its actions are the actions of men. It

is a salutary principle, a principle of law, that politicians who embark upon a particular policy – as here – of aggressive war should not be able to seek immunity behind the intangible personality of the state. It is a salutary legal rule that persons who, in violation of the law, plunge their own and other countries into an aggressive war should do so with a halter around their necks.'

In his most devastating attack on the defendants, Shawcross defined their responsibility:

'It may be said that many of the documents which have been referred to were in Hitler's name, and that the orders were Hitler's orders, and that these men were mere instruments of Hitler's will. But they were the instruments without which Hitler's will could not be carried out; and they were more than that. These men were no mere willing tools ... these are the men whose initiative and planning often conceived and certainly made possible the acts of aggression done in Hitler's name ... these are the men who enabled Hitler to build up the Army, the Navy, the Air Force, the war economy, the political philosophy, by which these treacherous attacks were carried out, and by which he was able to lead his fanatical followers into peaceful countries to murder, to loot, and to destroy. They are the men whose cooperation and support made the Nazi Government of Germany possible.'

Although his address was brief and low-key when compared with that of Robert Jackson, Sir Hartley Shawcross had effectively rubbished one of the key positions of the defence counsel: that from a legal standpoint, no crimes had been committed by the defendants.

Crimes against humanity

On 11 December, Thomas Dodd presented the American case for conspiracy to commit crimes against humanity. He began with the issue of forced labour, submitting:

'evidence concerning the conspirators' criminal deportation and enslavement of foreign labour, their illegal use of prisoners of war, their infamous concentration camps, and their relentless persecution of the Jews ... These crimes were committed both before and after Nazi Germany had launched her series of aggressions. They were committed within Germany and in foreign countries as well.'

Dodd announced that he would show how defendants Sauckel and Speer were instrumental 'for the formulation of the policy and for its execution'.

He drew on evidence found in a letter sent from Sauckel to Alfred Rosenberg in April 1942, which made the policy abundantly clear:

'The aim of this new, gigantic labour mobilization is to use all the rich and tremendous sources, conquered and secured for us by our fighting Armed Forces under the leadership of Adolf Hitler, for the armament of the Armed Forces and also for the nutrition of the homeland. The raw materials as well as the fertility of the conquered territories and their human labor power are to be used completely and conscientiously to the profit of Germany and her allies.'

Even more damning was a speech made by Erich Koch, commissar of Ukraine, in March 1943:

'I will draw the very last out of this country. I did not come to spread bliss. I have come to help the Führer. The population must work, work, and work again . . . for some people are getting excited that the population may not get enough to eat. The population cannot demand that ... We definitely did not come here to give out manna. We have come here to create the basis for victory ... We are a master race, which must remember that the lowliest German worker is racially and biologically a thousand times more valuable than the population here.'

Examples were cited of foreign slave labourers being used in the Krupp armament factories and of their appalling maltreatment. Dodd cited a bleak affidavit by a Dr Wilhelm Jaeger, who worked as a medical supervisor overseeing all of the Krupp workers' camps in the Essen region, which were manned by deported Eastern Europeans.

> 'Conditions in these camps was [sic] extremely bad ... The diet prescribed for the Eastern Workers was altogether insufficient; they were given 1,000 calories a day less than the minimum prescribed for any German. Moreover, while German workers engaged in the heaviest work received 5,000 calories a day, the Eastern Workers with comparable jobs received only 2,000 calories.'

He described the food rationing that allowed only for 'a small quantity of meat per week. Only inferior meats rejected by the veterinary, such as horse meat or tuberculin-infested, was [sic] permitted for this purpose.'

Perhaps the most chilling words came from SS leader Heinrich Himmler, who articulated clearly how little he cared for the well-being of the Nazis' slave labour force:

> 'What happens to the Russians, to the Czechs, does not interest me in the slightest. What the nations can offer in the way of good blood of our type we will take, if necessary, by kidnapping their children and raising them here with us. Whether the other nations live in prosperity or starve to death interests me only insofar as we need them as slaves for our culture; otherwise, it is of no interest to me. Whether 10,000 Russian females fall down from exhaustion while digging an anti-tank ditch or not interests me only insofar as the anti-tank ditch for Germany is finished.'

On 13 December Dodd moved on to discuss the concentration camps. As expected, the evidence provided was brutal. One piece of evidence that stood out came from the testimony of a liberated prisoner, who noted the fate of some tattooed inmates:

'After the tattooed prisoners had been examined, the ones with the best and most artistic specimens were kept in the dispensary and then killed by injections ... The corpses were then turned over to the pathological department where the desired pieces of tattooed skin were detached from the bodies and treated. The finished products were turned over to SS Standartenfuehrer Koch's wife, who had them fashioned into lampshades and other ornamental household articles.'

Dodd was able to show examples to the horrified courtroom, along with the shrunken head of a Polish officer that Koch, commandant of the Buchenwald concentration camp, used as a paperweight on his desk. Koch's behaviour would eventually be deemed too transgressive even for the Nazis: he was eventually shot by an SS firing squad when it was discovered that he had been embezzling property stolen from prisoners and had ordered the murder of a camp doctor who had been treating him for syphilis. His wife, Ilse – known to inmates as *Die Hexe von Buchenwald* (The Witch of Buchenwald) – would later become a notorious figure after accounts of her sadistic treatment of prisoners became known to the public.

Three witnesses

Much of the American conspiracy case presented during December 1945 was devoted either to Nazi treaty violations against those territories they had occupied – or had attempted to occupy – or organizations such as the Gestapo, the SS, the SA and the Leadership Corps, which also formed a large part of the business of the International Military Tribunal. On 3 January 1946 – the 26th day of the trial – the American prosecutors called the first of three prize witnesses, each one of whom had been detained along with the individual defendants – and who might just as easily have been on trial themselves.

SS Lieutenant General Otto Ohlendorf was brought to the stand to give evidence against Dr Ernst Kaltenbrunner, under whom he had served in the Reich Main Security Office. His interrogator was Colonel John Amen, an associate American trial counsel. The head of one of the four *Einsatzgruppen* – SS 'death squads' – during Operation Barbarossa, Hitler's invasion of the Soviet Union, Ohlendorf shocked the courtroom with his matter-of-fact responses.

[Amen]: Do you know how many persons were liquidated by Einsatz Group D under your direction?

[Ohlendorf]: In the year between June 1941 to June 1942 the Einsatzkommandos reported 90,000 people liquidated.

[Amen]: Did that include men, women, and children?

[Ohlendorf]: Yes.

Questioned about how he felt about ordering the killings, he struggled to comprehend the question.

'To me it is inconceivable that a subordinate leader should not carry out orders given by the leaders of the state.'

Ohlendorf was similarly brief when asked his thoughts on the legality of the orders: 'I do not understand your question; since the order was issued by the superior authorities, the question of legality could not arise in the minds of these individuals, for they had sworn obedience to the people who had issued the orders.'

Ohlendorf gave a chilling account of the mass executions he supervised:

'A local Einsatzkommando attempted to collect all the Jews in its area by registering them … on the pretext that they were to be resettled … from there they were later transported to the place of execution … the executions were carried out in a military manner, by firing squads under command ... the bodies were buried in the anti-tank ditch.'

When discussing the gas vans – the portable gas chambers in which 15 to 25 persons could be killed – Ohlendorf reported that 'the Einsatzkommandos did not willingly use the vans ... because the burial of the victims was a great ordeal'. Execution by shooting was, it seems, better for the mental health of his men.

SS captain Dieter Wisliceny had been Adolf Eichmann's deputy, so he had intimate knowledge of the *Judenfrage* ('The Jewish Question') and had seen Hitler's order to carry out the policy. Wisliceny was close friends with Eichmann: 'We used the intimate "*du*" and I also knew his family very well.' He confirmed the way in which the Nazi treatment of the Jews changed over time:

'Until 1940 the general policy within the section was to settle the Jewish question ... by means of a planned emigration. The second phase, after that date, was the concentration of all Jews ... in ghettos. This period lasted approximately until the beginning of 1942. The third period was the so-called "final solution" ... the planned extermination and destruction of the Jewish race. This period lasted until October 1944 when Himmler gave the order to stop their destruction.'

Requesting the verification of an order to transport Slovakian Jews to the Auschwitz extermination camp, Wisliceny claimed that Eichmann handed him a document saying:

'The Führer had ordered the final solution of the Jewish question; the Chief of the Security Police and the SD and the Inspector of Concentration Camps were entrusted with carrying out this so-called final solution. All Jewish men and women who were able to work were to be temporarily exempted from the so-called final solution and used for work in the concentration camps. This letter was signed by Himmler himself.'

Wisliceny continued:

> 'Eichmann went on to explain to me what was meant by this. He said that the planned biological annihilation of the Jewish race in the Eastern Territories was disguised by the concept and wording "final solution" … It was perfectly clear to me that this order spelled death to millions of people. I said to Eichmann, "God grant that our enemies never have the opportunity of doing the same to the German people", in reply to which Eichmann told me not to be sentimental.'

Wisliceny's testimony was so frank and explicit that neither the prosecutors nor the defence counsels felt the need for further questions.

SS Obergruppenführer Erich von dem Bach-Zelewski had drawn praise from Hitler himself for his supposed ruthlessness – even if US judge Biddle described him as looking like a 'mild and rather serious accountant'. Bach-Zelewski had been in charge of the anti-partisan units and reported directly to Heinrich Himmler. He caused consternation among the defendants when answering a question from American prosecutor Colonel Taylor about 'excessive' measures taken by his soldiers during anti-partisan activities:

> [Colonel Taylor]: Was an order ever issued by the highest authorities, that German soldiers who committed offenses against the civilian population were not to be punished in the military courts?

> [Bach-Zelewski]: Yes, this order was issued.

> [Colonel Taylor]: Did you report these excessive measures to the commanders of the army groups and other Wehrmacht officers with whom you worked?

> [Bach-Zelewski]: This state of affairs was generally known. There was no necessity to make a special report about it, since every

operation had immediately to be reported in all detail, and was known to every responsible leader.

The defendants were outraged. As Bach-Zelewski left the stand Göring called out to him: '*Schweinehund*! You damned traitor!' By some accounts he later described him as 'the bloodiest murderer of the whole damn set-up'.

In spite of acting as significant prosecution witnesses at Nuremberg, both Ohlendorf and Wisliceny would find themselves convicted at later war trials and were both ultimately hanged for their crimes. Bach-Zelewski remained free until 1958, when he was imprisoned for murders he committed in the 1930s. He died in prison in 1972.

The defendants

On 8 January 1946 the charges against individual defendants began. Three of those on trial – Sauckel, Speer and Kaltenbrunner – were excluded from this since the prosecution felt that their guilt had been well enough established by means of earlier evidence on slave labour (Sauckel and Speer) and 'criminal organizations'. That is, the Gestapo and the SS (Kaltenbrunner). Furthermore, some of the presentations, such as those against Keitel, Jodl, Papen, Schirach, Bormann and Neurath largely comprised evidence that had already been presented earlier, in the general prosecutions against 'illegal' organizations.

Hermann Göring

As the Allies' prize Nazi captive, it came as little surprise to find voluminous documentary evidence offered against Hermann Göring. Charged on all four indictments, the presentation was given by Ralph Albrecht, a US associate trial counsel, beginning with a damning assessment of the defendant's background, describing him as 'perhaps the most important conspirator on trial'. He was, Albrecht continued:

'The Number Two Nazi, the Nazi who stood next to the Führer himself, the Nazi who was in some respects even more dangerous than the Führer … because, unlike many leading

Nazis, including Hitler, who were morally and socially on the fringes of society before the Nazi Party rode to success in 1933, this conspirator was known to come of substantial family which had furnished officers to the army and important civil servants to the country in the past.'

Albrecht continued with this personal line of attack:

'Moreover, he was possessed of substantial appearance, an ingratiating manner, a certain affability. But all of these facets of character were but deceptions, because they helped to conceal the man's core of steel, his vindictiveness, his cruelty, his lust for self-adornment, self-glorification, and power … Much of the benevolence of this conspirator, his ever-ready smile and ingratiating manner, were daily in evidence in this chamber. His ready affirmation, by a pleasant nod for all to see, of the correctness of statements made or the contents of documents offered by counsel, his chiding shake of the head when he disagreed with such facts were commonplace.'

Visibly irritated by this personal detail, presiding judge Sir Geoffrey Lawrence stepped in: 'I don't think the Tribunal is interested in this, Mr. Albrecht.' Albrecht then moved on to presenting the evidence.

'For more than two decades Goering's activities extended over nearly every phase of the conspiracy. He was one of the conspirators associated with Hitler from the very beginning. A member of the Party since 1922, he participated in the Munich Putsch of November 1923 at the head of the SA, a Nazi organization shown to have been committed to the use of violence … Goering has frequently and proudly acknowledged his personal responsibility for the crimes committed pursuant to orders of this character, and I recall his words which he uttered before thousands of his fellow Germans: "Each bullet which leaves the barrel of a police pistol now is my bullet. If

one calls this murder, then I have murdered; I ordered all this,
I back it up."'

Albrecht continued to provide evidence establishing how even Hitler
himself had spoken of Göring's central role in the Nazi Party, and how
he had 'boasted that no title and no decoration could make him so
proud as the designation given to him by the German people ... "the
most faithful paladin of our Führer".'

Colonel Albrecht concluded with what he described as a 'fitting
climax', a letter that Göring had written to the 'notorious' Reinhard
Heydrich, the main architect of the Holocaust:

'Complementing the task that was assigned to you on 24 January
1939 which dealt with arriving at – through furtherance of
emigration and evacuation – a solution of the Jewish problem,
as advantageously as possible, I hereby charge you to make all
necessary organizational and practical preparations for bringing
about a complete solution of the Jewish question in the German
sphere of influence in Europe ... I charge you furthermore to send
me, before long, an overall plan concerning the organizational,
factual, and material measures necessary for the accomplishment
of the desired final solution of the Jewish question.'

Joachim von Ribbentrop

The British prosecutor Sir David Maxwell Fyfe presented the case
against Ribbentrop. Charged on all four indictments, documentary
evidence against Ribbentrop was offered on each count, although it
largely comprised documentation that had been used earlier in the
general prosecutions. He was accused of being directly responsible for
atrocities that took place in Denmark and Vichy France, since officials
in those territories reported directly to him. As German Foreign Minister,
Ribbentrop had played a vital role in brokering the so-called 'Pact of
Steel' with Mussolini in Italy and the later *Anschluss* – the annexation of
Austria. Hitler was quoted in the evidence: 'In the historic year of 1938
the Foreign Minister, von Ribbentrop, was of great help to me by virtue

of his accurate and audacious judgment and admirably clever treatment of all problems of foreign policy.'

Alfred Rosenberg

The case against Rosenberg was presented by 31-year-old United States assistant trial counsel Walter W. Brudno – at that time still holding the rank of private in the US Army. Rosenberg had already been heavily implicated in the infamous looting of artworks, the 'Nazi Plunder' – he even had a taskforce devoted to appropriating cultural property named after him, the Einsatzstab Reichsleiter Rosenberg. Here, though, Brudno placed more emphasis on the influence of Rosenberg's early writings, in particular his book *The Myth of the Twentieth Century* – so much so that Tribunal President Lawrence interrupted with a terse 'we really don't want to hear any more about it'. Brudno was nevertheless able to emphasize Rosenberg's importance in Nazi ideology by reading the citation that accompanied his award of the 1937 German National Prize: 'Alfred Rosenberg has helped with his publications to lay the scientific and intuitive foundation and to strengthen the ideology of National Socialism in the most excellent way.'

Rosenberg had also founded the *Institut zur Erforschung der Judenfrage* (Institute for Research of the Jewish Question). Brudno quoted from a damning statement reported in the press on its opening:

> 'For Germany the Jewish question is only then solved when the last Jew has left the Greater German space … Since Germany with its blood and its folkdom has now broken for always this Jewish dictatorship for all Europe and has seen to it that Europe as a whole will become free from the Jewish parasitism once more, we may, I believe, also say for all Europeans: For Europe the Jewish question is only then solved when the last Jew has left the European continent.'

Referring to earlier evidence, Brudno continued: 'It has already been seen that Rosenberg did not overlook any opportunity to put these anti-Semitic beliefs into practice.'

The prosecutor also presented evidence regarding Rosenberg's influence on the education of Nazi youth:

'In his capacity as the Führer's delegate for the spiritual and ideological training, Rosenberg assisted in the preparation of the curriculum for the Adolf Hitler schools. These schools, it will be recalled, selected the most suitable candidates from the Hitler Jugend and trained them for leadership within the Party. They were the elite schools of National Socialism.'

Dr Hans Frank

Colonel William H. Baldwin presented evidence against Hans Frank. Once Hitler's personal lawyer, Frank had been Governor General of Occupied Poland and had instituted a reign of terror against its civilian population. Following his arrest he handed his captors 43 volumes of the diaries that he had maintained throughout the war. Frank hoped that the periodic criticisms of Hitler within their pages would buy him favour with the Allies but the diaries were, instead, used by the prosecution against him. Baldwin quoted from them extensively.

'As a National Socialist I was a participant in the events of November 1923, for which I received the Order of the Blood. After the resurrection of the movement in the year 1925, my really greater activity in the movement began, which made me, first gradually, later almost exclusively, the legal adviser of the Führer and of the Reich Party Directorate of the NSDAP. I was thus the representative of the legal interests of the growing Third Reich in a legal-ideological as well as in a practical way ... The culmination of this work I see in the Leipzig army trial, in which I succeeded in having the Führer admitted to the famous oath of legality, a circumstance which gave the Movement legal grounds to expand on a large scale. The Führer, indeed, recognized this achievement and in 1926 made me leader of the National Socialist Lawyers' League; in 1929, Reichsleiter of the Reich Legal Office of the NSDAP; in March 1933, Bavarian Minister of Justice; in the same year, Reich Commissioner for Justice; in 1934, President of the Academy of German Law, founded by me; and in December 1934, Reich Minister without Portfolio. And in 1939, I was finally appointed Governor General for the occupied Polish territories ... I profess myself, now and always, as a National Socialist and a faithful follower of the Führer, Adolf Hitler, whom I have now served since 1919.'

Julius Streicher

Like Frank, Streicher condemned himself with his own words, which were published and read by tens of thousands of Germans. Described by the British prosecutor Lieutenant Colonel M.G. Griffith Jones as 'Jew-baiter Number One' and as editor and publisher of the newspaper *Der Stürmer*: 'for the course of some 25 years this man educated the whole of the German people in hatred and incited them to the persecution and to the extermination of the Jewish race. He was an accessory to murder, perhaps on a scale never attained before.'

The prosecution gave endless examples of Streicher's inflammatory rhetoric, beginning with extracts from the mid-1920s:

'The Jew seeks domination not only among the German people but among all peoples ... Do you not know that the God of the Old Testament ordered the Jews to devour and enslave the peoples of the earth? ... The Government allows the Jew to do as he pleases. The people expect action to be taken ... You may think about Adolf Hitler as you please, but one thing you must admit. He possessed the courage to attempt to free the German people from the Jew by a national revolution. That was a great deed ... You must realize that the Jew wants our people to perish ... That is why you must join us and leave those who have brought you nothing but war and inflation and discord. For thousands of years the Jew has been destroying the nations ... Let us start today, so that we can annihilate the Jews.'

A letter published in *Der Stürmer* in April 1937 perhaps topped the other evidence against him. It came from head of the SS Heinrich Himmler, who proudly declared:

> 'When in future years the history of the reawakening of the German people is written and the next generation is already unable to understand that the German people were once friendly to the Jews, it will be recognized that Julius Streicher and his weekly paper *Der Stürmer* contributed a great deal toward the enlightenment regarding the enemy of mankind.'

Hjalmar Schacht and Walther Funk

Economist Schacht had been president of the Reichsbank from the time of the Nazi takeover in 1933 until 1939, when he was succeeded by Walther Funk. By its own admission, the prosecution's case against Schacht was weaker than for any other defendant:

> 'Schacht's control over the German economy was on the wane after November 1937 ... We know too that he is sometimes credited with opposition to certain of the more radical elements of the Nazi Party; and I further understand that at the time of capture by United States forces he was under German detention in a prison camp, having been arrested by the Gestapo in July 1944.'

Charges against him were based on his influence as Minister of Economics. Schacht was

> 'the dominant figure in the rearming of Germany and in the economic planning and preparation for war; that without his work the Nazis would not have been able to wring from their depressed economy the tremendous material requirements of armed aggression; and that Schacht contributed his efforts with full knowledge of the aggressive purposes which he was serving.'

Indeed, the prosecution offered examples of complex, 'ingenious and often ruthless devices' by which Schacht helped to reboot a failing German economy in the 1930s

> '[by] negotiating stand-still agreements, forcing payment in Reichsmark of interest and amortization on debts incurred in foreign currency, using scrip and funding bonds for the same purpose, suspending service on foreign-held debts, blocking foreign-held marks, freezing foreign claims in Germany, eliminating unessential foreign expenditures, requisitioning German-held foreign exchange, subsidizing exports, issuing restricted marks, bartering under clearing agreements, licensing imports, and controlling all foreign exchange transactions to the end of favoring raw materials for armaments.'

(Schacht, who held a PhD and had studied medicine, philology and political sciences at the universities of Munich, Leipzig, Berlin, Paris and Kiel, had scored the 'genius-level' IQ of 143 when examined by American prison psychologists.)

Although Schacht's successor, Walther Funk, had been branded by Robert Jackson as 'The Banker of Gold Teeth' – referring to the practice of producing bullion from melting down gold teeth extracted from concentration camp victims – most of the conspiracy evidence offered was from his work in the Ministry of Public Enlightenment and Propaganda. Once again, however, the accusations against Funk seemed relatively pale when compared to the charges of mass murder being levelled against others on trial. Indeed, Göring himself dismissed Funk as 'an insignificant subordinate'.

Dr Franz Blaha (witness)

Following the conclusion of the conspiracy case against Funk, US prosecutor Thomas Dodd introduced the first concentration camp witness, Franz Blaha, a Czech doctor who on 11 January 1946 gave a harrowing – not to mention horrifyingly detailed – account of activities at the Dachau concentration camp where he was interned from 1941 until its liberation in April 1945. In his affidavit, he reported:

'From the middle of 1941 to the end of 1942 some 500 operations on healthy prisoners were performed. These were for the instruction of the SS medical students and doctors and included operations on the stomach, gall bladder, and throat. These were performed by students and doctors of only two years' training, although they were very dangerous and difficult. Ordinarily they would not have been done except by surgeons with at least four years' surgical practice. Many prisoners died on the operating table and many others from later complications. I performed autopsies on all of these bodies ...

'During my time at Dachau I was familiar with many kinds of medical experiments carried on there on human victims. These persons were never volunteers but were forced to submit to such acts. Malaria experiments on about 1,200 people were conducted by Dr. Klaus Schilling between 1941 and 1945. Schilling was personally ordered by Himmler to conduct these experiments. The victims were either bitten by mosquitoes or given injections of malaria sporozoites taken from mosquitoes ... I performed autopsies on the bodies of people who died from these malaria experiments. Thirty to forty died from the malaria itself. Three hundred to four hundred died later from diseases which were fatal because of the physical condition resulting from the malaria attacks. In addition there were deaths resulting from poisoning due to overdoses of neosalvarsan and pyramidon ...

'In 1942 and 1943 experiments on human beings were conducted by Dr. Sigmund Rascher to determine the effects of changing air pressure. As many as 25 persons were put at one time into a specially constructed van in which pressure could be increased or decreased as required. The purpose was to find out the effects on human beings of high altitude and of rapid descents by parachute. Through a window in the van I have seen the people lying on the floor of the van ... Most of the prisoners used died from these experiments, from internal haemorrhage of the lungs or brain. The survivors coughed blood when taken out. It was my job to take the bodies out and as soon as they were found to be dead to send the internal organs to Munich for study. About 400 to 500 prisoners were experimented on. The survivors were sent to invalid blocks and liquidated shortly afterwards. Only a few escaped.

'Rascher also conducted experiments on the effect of cold water on human beings. This was done to find a way for reviving airmen who had fallen into the ocean. The subject was placed in ice cold water and kept there until he was unconscious ... Some men stood it as long as 24 to 36 hours. The lowest body temperature reached was 19 degrees centigrade, but most men died at 25 or 26 degrees. When the men were removed from the ice water attempts were made to revive them by artificial sunshine, with hot water, by electro-therapy, or by animal warmth. For this last experiment prostitutes were used and the body of the unconscious man was placed between the bodies of two women. Himmler was present at one such experiment ... About 300 persons were used in these experiments. The majority died. Of those who survived, many became mentally deranged. Those who did not die were sent to invalid blocks and were killed just as were the victims of the air pressure experiments ...

'It was common practice to remove the skin from dead prisoners. I was commanded to do this on many occasions ... It was chemically treated and placed in the sun to dry. After that it was cut into various sizes for use as saddles, riding breeches, gloves, house slippers, and ladies' handbags. Tattooed skin was especially valued by SS men ... This skin had to be from healthy prisoners and free from defects. Sometimes we did not have enough bodies with good skin ... Also we frequently got requests for the skulls or skeletons of prisoners. In those cases we boiled the skull or the body. Then the soft parts were removed and the bones were bleached and dried and reassembled.

'Many executions by gas or shooting or injections took place right in the camp. The gas chamber was completed in 1944, and I was called by Dr. Rascher to examine the first victims. Of the eight or nine persons in the chamber there were three still alive, and the remainder appeared to be dead. Their eyes were red, and their faces were swollen. Many prisoners were later killed in this way. Afterwards they were removed to the crematorium where I had to examine their teeth for gold. Teeth containing gold were extracted.'

(This point in Dr Blaha's statement would be disputed by some, who claimed that there were no gas chambers at Dachau concentration camp, thus bringing other aspects of his testimony into question.)

The most dramatic happening during Dr Blaha's testimony came when he was asked by prosecutor Dodd if he could identify visitors to the Dachau camp in the courtroom and describe those visits. Blaha was able to pick out Frick, Rosenberg, Funk, Sauckel and Kaltenbrunner from the defendants' box, and also recalled that the absent Bormann had been seen at Dachau.

Under cross-examination from French prosecutor Dubost, Blaha's testimony crossed into uncharted territory when he was asked: 'Can you say if any ordinary people, like workers or farmers, knew what was going on in this camp?'

Blaha replied:

'In my opinion the people who lived in the neighborhood of Munich must have known of all these things, because the prisoners went every day to various factories in Munich and the neighborhood; and at work they frequently came into contact with the civilian workers. Moreover, the various suppliers and consumers often entered the fields and the factories of the German armament works and they saw what was done to the prisoners and what they looked like.'

Karl Dönitz and Erich Raeder

Grossadmiral, or grand admiral, was the highest rank in the navy of Nazi Germany. Admiral Erich Raeder was appointed to the position in 1939 before being replaced in 1943 by Admiral Karl Dönitz. When the selection of prisoners to face prosecution was being made there was considerable disagreement among the Allies as to whether these two naval leaders should stand trial. Indeed, the presentation of incriminating evidence, in particular against Dönitz, sometimes seemed to resemble a list of impressive military achievements.

However, the prosecution produced evidence of ruthless top secret orders that Dönitz had sent to his U-boat commanders in September 1942:

'No attempt of any kind must be made at rescuing members of ships sunk ... this includes picking up persons in the water and putting them in lifeboats, righting capsized lifeboats and handing over food and water. Rescue runs counter to the rudimentary demands of warfare for the destruction of enemy ships and crews ... Rescue the shipwrecked only if their statements will be of importance to your boat ... Be harsh, having in mind that the enemy takes no regard of women and children in his bombing attacks on German cities.'

At this point, testimonies from two witnesses, former U-boat commanders Peter Heisig and Karl-Heinz Moehle, were introduced. In spite of careful cross-examination by the defence counsel, both seemed to be confirming the veracity of the order.

Further evidence against Dönitz – in his own words – related to the use of slave labour in German shipyards to replace heavy shipping losses:

'I propose reinforcing the shipyard working parties by prisoners from the concentration camps, and as a special measure for relieving the present shortage of coppersmiths, especially in U-boat construction, I propose to divert coppersmiths from the reduced construction of locomotives to shipbuilding ... 12,000 concentration camp prisoners will be employed in the shipyards as additional labour.'

British junior prosecution counsel Colonel Harry J. Phillimore summed up the case against Dönitz:

'The defendant was no plain sailor, playing the part of a service officer, loyally obedient to the orders of the government of the day; he was an extreme Nazi who did his utmost to indoctrinate the Navy and the German people with the Nazi creed. It is no coincidence that it was he who was chosen to succeed Hitler; not Göring, not Ribbentrop, not Goebbels, not Himmler.

'He played a big part in fashioning the U-Boat fleet, one of the most deadly weapons of aggressive war. He helped to plan and execute aggressive war, and we cannot doubt that he knew well that these wars were in deliberate violation of treaties ... He was ready to order, and did order, the murder of helpless survivors of sunken ships, an action only paralleled by that of his Japanese ally ... there can be few countries where widows or parents do not mourn for men of the merchant navies whose destruction was due to the callous brutality with which – at the orders of this man – the German U-Boats did their work.'

British junior counsel Major Elwyn Jones proceeded to give evidence against Admiral Raeder, 'the creator of the Nazi Navy'. Much was made of his role in German rearmament, contrary to the terms of the Treaty of Versailles, and documentary evidence was offered that he had been instrumental in convincing Hitler to occupy Norway.

Wilhelm Frick

The conspiracy case against Wilhelm Frick was presented by American assistant trial counsel Dr Robert M.W. Kempner on 16 January 1946, the 35th day of the trial. Frick was, Kempner began: 'The administrative brain who devised the machinery of state for Nazism, who geared that machinery for aggressive war.' First, he asked the Tribune to note that Frick had received 'favourable mention' in no less a tome than Adolf Hitler's *Mein Kampf*. And second, that in a treason document prepared by the Prussian Ministry of the Interior in 1930: 'It states that Frick, next to Hitler, can be regarded as the most influential representative of the Nazi Party.'

When Hitler was appointed Chancellor of Germany by President von Hindenburg in 1933, Frick and Hermann Göring were the only two Nazi Reich Ministers in Hitler's original cabinet. At this time, Kempner argued:

'Frick used his wide powers as Reich Minister of the Interior to advance the cause of the Nazi conspiracy. To accomplish this purpose, he drafted and signed the laws and decrees which abolished the autonomous state governments, the autonomous local governments, and the political parties in Germany other than the Nazi Party.'

Kempner further quoted from a book written by Frick's undersecretary, Hans Pfundtner:

'While Marxism in Prussia was crushed by the hard fist of the Prussian Prime Minister Hermann Göring and a gigantic wave of propaganda was initiated for the Reichstag elections of 5 March 1933, Dr. Frick prepared the complete seizure of power in all states of the Reich. All at once the political opposition disappeared ... from this time on only one will and one leadership reigned in the German Reich.'

The end of Kempner's presentation signalled the conclusion of the evidence of conspiracy (the first indictment) presented by the American prosecutors, which had also included the far briefer British presentation for the second indictment. The French and Russian teams now prepared to present their cases on the third and fourth indictments – war crimes and crimes against humanity.

CHAPTER 6

War Crimes and Crimes Against Humanity

At the beginning of the morning session of 17 January 1946 – the 36th day of the trial – François de Menthon came to the lectern to make the opening statement on behalf of the French prosecution. He gave an impassioned performance lasting more than four hours.

> 'The conscience of the peoples, who only yesterday were enslaved and tortured both in soul and body, calls upon you to judge and to condemn the most monstrous attempt at domination and barbarism of all times, both in the persons of some of those who bear the chief responsibility and in the collective groups and organizations which were the essential instruments of their crimes.'

Menthon's opening took a deliberately emotive line, evoking the spirit of the resistance movement that continued the fight following the arrival of the Nazis, in which, indeed, he had himself played a role:

> 'France, invaded twice in 30 years in the course of wars, both of which were launched by German imperialism, bore almost alone in May and June 1940 the weight of armaments accumulated by Nazi Germany over a period of years in a spirit of aggression. Although temporarily crushed by superiority in numbers,

material, and preparation, my country never gave up the battle for freedom ... Our people refused not only to submit to wretchedness and slavery, but even more they refused to accept the Hitlerian dogmas which were in absolute contradiction to their traditions, their aspirations, and their human calling.

'France, which was systematically plundered and ruined; France, so many of whose sons were tortured and murdered in the jails of the Gestapo or in concentration camps; France, which was subjected to the still more horrible grip of demoralization and return to barbarism diabolically imposed by Nazi Germany, asks you, above all in the name of the heroic martyrs of the Resistance, who are among the greatest heroes of our national legend, that justice be done.

'We shall expose the various aspects of this policy of criminality as it was pursued in the occupied countries of Western Europe, by dealing successively with Forced Labour, Economic Looting, Crimes against Persons, and Crimes against Mankind ... Germany proposed to utilize to the maximum the labour potential of the enslaved populations in order to maintain the German war production at the necessary level.'

Like the American prosecution, Menthon had evoked the German violation of the 1928 Kellogg–Briand Pact – an international agreement in which signatories (among them Germany) promised not to use war to resolve disputes or conflicts:

'Acts committed in the execution of a war are assaults on persons and goods which are themselves prohibited but are sanctioned in all legislations. The state of war could make them legitimate only if the war itself was legitimate. Inasmuch as this is no longer the case, since the Kellogg–Briand Pact, these acts become purely and simply common law crimes. As Mr. Justice Jackson has already argued before you with irrefutable logic, any recourse to war is a recourse to means which are in themselves criminal.'

Although Menthon's lengthy speech was at times overwrought, it largely maintained focus on the legal arguments against Germany's war crimes and crimes against humanity. The French prosecution, however, differed from that of Britain and America in that it made no distinction between the Nazis and the people of Germany:

'These people have been for many years intoxicated by Nazism; certain of their eternal and deep-seated aspirations, under this regime, have found a monstrous expression; their entire responsibility is involved, not only by their general acceptance but by the effective participation of a great number of them in the crimes committed. Their re-education is indispensable. This represents a difficult enterprise and one of long duration. The efforts which the free peoples will have to make in order to reintegrate Germany into an international community cannot succeed in the end if this re-education is not carried out effectively.

'... The truly diabolical enterprise of Hitler and of his companions was to assemble in a body of dogmas formed around the concept of race, all the instincts of barbarism, repressed by centuries of civilization, but always present in men's innermost nature, all the negations of the traditional values of humanity, on which nations, as well as individuals, question their conscience in the troubled hours of their development and of their life; to construct and to propagate a doctrine which organizes, regulates, and aspires to command crime.'

Menthon concluded his opening with an impassioned plea for the justice of the victims:

'Your judgment must be inscribed as a decisive act in the history of international law in order to prepare the establishment of a true international society excluding recourse to war and enlisting force permanently in the service of the justice of nations; it will be one of the foundations of this peaceful order to which nations aspire on the morrow of this frightful torment. The need for justice of the martyred peoples will be satisfied, and their sufferings will not have been useless to the progress of mankind.'

Forced labour

The French evidence focused firmly on facts and statistics found within more than 800 seized Nazi documents. It began with presentations on forced labour, not only in France but in Denmark, Norway and the Netherlands. Assistant French Prosecutor Jacques B. Herzog began by describing the nature of labour under National Socialism. Quoting from an unnamed German writer, he told the courtroom that it was, 'not a simple judicial relationship between the worker and his employer; it is a living phenomenon in which the worker becomes a cog in the National Socialist machine for collective production. The conception of compulsory labour is thus, for National Socialism, necessarily complementary to the conception of work itself.'

The use of forced labour in conquered territories violated a number of international agreements, not least, as far as Germany and France were concerned, the Franco-German Armistice signed in 1940 after the Nazi invasion. Herzog presented damning statistics from official reports:

'738,000 workers were pressed into compulsory labor service in France; 875,952 French workers were deported to German factories; 987,687 prisoners of war were utilized for the Reich war economy. A total of 2,601,639 workers of French citizenship thus were pressed into work serving the war effort of National Socialist Germany.'

This was supplemented by 150,000 Belgians and 431,400 Dutch. Quoting from a speech at the 43rd conference of Hitler's four-year economic plan, Herzog reported that Sauckel had claimed 'that there were 5 million foreign workers in Germany, of whom 200,000 were actually volunteers'. Furthermore, Seyss-Inquart was implicated in providing Sauckel with forced labour from Belgium and the Netherlands since he

Jewish men are transported from the Warsaw Ghetto by Wehrmacht soldiers,
to work as slaves.

had 'introduced the compulsory labour service in the Netherlands by an ordinance of 28 February 1941', and in Belgium on 23 March 1942.

> 'The Defendant Seyss-Inquart has thus paved the way on which the Defendant Sauckel was to be enabled to proceed to action. Sauckel actually utilized all the human potential of the Netherlands. New measures were soon necessary – measures which Seyss-Inquart adopted.'

Herzog then quoted a 1943 ordnance that 'ordered the mobilization of all men from 18 to 35 years of age'.

Economic pillaging

A large portion of the French evidence was in the area of Nazi looting and economic pillaging in the occupied territories. The presentation went on for days in which document after document recorded the extent of illegal seizures:

> 'The Germans imposed the costs of billeting their troops upon Belgium. Having done this, the occupation authorities justified themselves by a rather liberal interpretation of Article 52 of the Hague Convention, according to the provisions of which the occupying power may require levies in kind and in services ... Belgium had to meet expenses to the amount of 5,900 million francs for billeting costs, equipment, and furniture ... According to Article 53 of the Hague Convention, the occupying army has the right to seize means of transport and communications provided that it returns them and pays indemnity. That army, however, does not possess the right to make the occupied country pay the costs of transport put at the army's disposal. That is, however, what Germany did in Belgium.'

The Nazis used the same ordnance in other occupied territories of Western Europe, where transport and communications material were seized. In the Netherlands, for example:

'Railways – of 890 locomotives, 490 were requisitioned; of 30,000 freight cars, 28,950 were requisitioned; of 1,750 passenger cars, 1,446 were requisitioned; of 300 electric trains, 215 were requisitioned ... In general, the little material left by the Germans was badly damaged either by wear and tear, by military operations, or by sabotage ... the Germans seized the greater part of the motorcars, motorcycles, and about one million bicycles. They left the population only those machines which would not run.'

The Nazis also stripped the transport infrastructure of The Hague and Rotterdam, transporting it to German cities: 'Some 50 tramcars with motors and 42 trailers were sent to Bremen and Hamburg. A considerable amount of rails, cables, and other accessories were removed and transported to Germany. The motor buses of the tramway companies were likewise taken by the occupying power.'

And agricultural produce was taken. In Norway, for instance: 'Meat, 30,000 tons; dairy products and eggs, 61,000 tons; fish, 26,000 tons; fruit and vegetables, 68,000 tons; potatoes, 500,000 tons; beverages and vinegar, 112,000 tons; fats, 10,000 tons; wheat and flour, 3,000 tons; other foodstuffs, 5,000 tons; hay and straw, 300,000 tons.'

As French prosecutor Charles Gerthoffer noted, this created severe deprivation among the occupied peoples:

'In France particularly, many persons died solely because of undernourishment ... It was estimated that people require from 3,000 to 3,500 calories a day and heavy labourers about 4,000. From the beginning of the rationing in September 1940 only 1,800 calories per day per person were distributed. Successively the ration decreased to 1,700 calories in 1942, then to 1,500, and finally fell to 1,220 and 900 calories a day for adults ... old persons were given only 850 calories a day. The Germans could not fail to recognize the disastrous situation as far as public health was concerned, since they themselves estimated in the course of the war of 1914–1918 that the distribution of 1,700 calories a day was a "regime of slow starvation, leading to death".'

Harrowing testimony

From 23 January to 7 February, following further cases against Fritzsche, Papen and Neurath – this time regarding Crimes Against Peace, War Crimes and Crimes Against Humanity – the French prosecutors began focusing in detail on what they categorized as 'Atrocities Committed in the Occupied Countries of the West'. On 25 January, French prosecutor Charles Dubost brought to the stand a witness named Maurice Lampe, a Frenchman who had been interred at the Mauthausen concentration camp. His testimony was typically harrowing:

'When we arrived at Mauthausen, the SS officer who received this convoy of about 1,200 Frenchmen informed us in the following words, which I shall quote from memory almost word for word: "Germany needs your arms. You are, therefore, going to work; but I want to tell you that you will never see your families again. When one enters this camp, one leaves it by the chimney of the crematorium." ... We started work at seven o'clock in the morning. By eight o'clock, one hour later, two of my comrades had already been murdered ... because they had not understood the order ... We were very frequently beaten because of our inability to understand the German language.'

Lampe related an incident of appalling barbarity that took place in September 1944:

'There came to Mauthausen a small convoy of 47 British, American, and Dutch officers. They were airmen who had come down by parachute ... Because of this they were condemned to death by a German tribunal. They had been in prison about a year and a half and were brought to Mauthausen for execution ... and were told by the commanding officer of the camp that they were all under sentence of death ... One of the American officers asked the commander that he should be allowed to meet his death as a soldier. In reply, he was bashed with a whip. The 47 were led barefoot to the quarry ... At the bottom of the steps they loaded stones on the backs of these poor men and they had to carry them to the top. The first journey was made with stones weighing 25 to 30 kilos and was accompanied by blows. Then they were made to run down. For the second journey the stones were still heavier; and whenever the poor wretches sank under their burden, they were kicked and hit with a bludgeon, and even stones were hurled at them.

'This went on for several days. In the evening when I returned from the gang with which I was then working, the road which led to the camp was a bath of blood. I almost stepped on the lower jaw of a man. Twenty-one bodies were strewn along the road. Twenty-one had died on the first day.'

The others, it seems, died the following day.

Lampe also related a visit to Mauthausen from Heinrich Himmler, who had been invited to witness the execution of 50 Soviet prisoners:

'The block where I was billeted was just opposite the crematorium ... in the execution room I saw these Soviet officers lined up in rows of five in front of my block ... They were called one by one, and there was a sort of human chain between the group which was awaiting its turn and that which was in the stairway listening to the shots which killed their predecessors. They were all killed by a shot in the neck ... we saw the condemned men who were waiting on the stairway opposite us embrace each other before they parted.'

Lampe made further shocking claims to the courtroom. In one instance, 400 prisoners were murdered because the camp was overcrowded. According to the witness, they were stripped naked, drenched in freezing water and left outside in temperatures of 18 degrees below zero. 'In the morning when the gangs went to work the corpses were strewn over the ground ... the last of them were finished off with blows from an axe.'

It was noted that during Lampe's testimony, given in French, a number of the defendants could not bear to listen and removed their earphones.

Prosecutor Dubost brought a second witness to the stand, with another typically grotesque tale to tell. Photojournalist Marie-Claude Vaillant-Couturier – so successful in a male-dominated industry that she had been known as 'the lady in Rolleiflex' – had been arrested by Marshal Pétain's Vichy French police and sent to Auschwitz.

'The work at Auschwitz consisted of clearing demolished houses, road building, and especially the draining of marsh land ... During the work the SS men and women who stood guard over us would beat us with cudgels and set their dogs on us. Many of our friends had their legs torn by the dogs. I even saw a woman torn to pieces and die under my very eyes when Tauber, a member of the SS, encouraged his dog to attack her and grinned at the sight.'

She described a particularly brutal roll call in February 1943:

'In the morning at 3:30 the whole camp was awakened and sent out on the plain ... We remained out in front of the camp until five in the afternoon, in the snow, without any food. Then when the signal was given we had to go through the door one by one, and we were struck in the back with a cudgel, each one of us, in order to make us run. Those who could not run, either because they were too old or too ill were caught by a hook and taken to Block 25, the "waiting block" for the gas chamber. On that day 10 of the French women of our convoy were thus caught and taken to Block 25.

'When all the internees were back in the camp, a party to which I belonged was organized to go and pick up the bodies of the dead which were scattered over the plain as on a battlefield. We carried to the yard of Block 25 the dead and the dying without distinction, and they remained there stacked up in a pile … one saw stacks of corpses piled up in the courtyard, and from time to time a hand or a head would stir among the bodies … It was a dying woman attempting to get free and live. The rate of mortality in that block was even more terrible than elsewhere because, having been condemned to death, they received food or drink only if there was something left in the cans in the kitchen; which means that very often they went for several days without a drop of water.'

Madame Vaillant-Couturier related a further incident of a young woman passing the block one day who was overcome by pity for the endless cries of thirst:

'She came back to our block to get a little herbal tea, but as she was passing it through the bars of the window she was seen by the *Aufseherin* [female concentration camp guard], who took her by the neck and threw her into Block 25 … Two days later I saw her on the truck which was taking the internees to the gas chamber. She had her arms around another French woman … when the truck started moving she cried, "Think of my little boy, if you ever get back to France." Then they started singing "The Marseillaise".'

During her testimony she also talked about medical experiments that took place at Auschwitz, having witnessed a 'queue of young Jewesses from Salonika who stood waiting in front of the X-ray room for sterilization … They sterilized women either by injections or by operation or with rays … There was a very high mortality rate among those operated upon.'

The French prosecutor next called a Dr Victor Dupont, who was deported from Paris to Buchenwald on 24 January 1944. He began his testimony:

'When I arrived at Buchenwald, I soon became aware of the difficult living conditions. The regime imposed upon the prisoners was not based on any principle of justice ... The interrogations which I underwent and which I saw others undergo were particularly inhuman.'

There was, he noted:

'Every imaginable kind of beating, immersion in bathtubs, squeezing of testicles, hanging, crushing of the head in iron bands, and the torturing of entire families in each others' sight. I have, in particular, seen a wife tortured before her husband; and children were tortured before their mothers ... Once in the camp, conditions were the same for everyone.'

Among the remaining French witnesses was Dr Alfred Balachowsky, a laboratory head at the noted Pasteur Institute in Paris. Balachowsky had been arrested in 1943 and sent to Buchenwald and then on to the Mittelbau-Dora Camp in the south of Germany, the top secret base for the building of the V-1 and V-2 rockets. He was able to talk of the medical experiments that took place at Block 45 in Buchenwald, where prisoners were most commonly 'used for observing the effects of drugs, poisons, bacterial cultures'. When the Nazis conducted experiments on the effectiveness of vaccines for typhus, healthy individuals were deliberately contaminated.

As a scientist, Balachowsky was scathing: 'The experiments carried out in Block 46 did without doubt serve a medical purpose, but for the greater part they were of no service to science. Therefore, they can hardly be called experiments.'

Dubost next called Hans Cappelen to the stand, where he spoke about the treatment of internees in camps and prisons in occupied Norway. He talked of his interrogation at the hands of the Nazis:

'They started in at once to beat me with bludgeons. How long this interrogation lasted I cannot remember, but it led to nothing

… I had to undress until I was absolutely naked. I was a little bit swollen after the first treatment … There were present about six or eight Gestapo agents and their leader … He was very angry and they started to bombard me with questions which I could not answer … [He] ran at me and tore all the hair off my head, hair and blood were all over the floor around me … All of a sudden, they all started to run at me and beat me with rubber bludgeons and iron cable-ends. That hurt me very badly and I fainted. But I was brought back to life again by their pouring ice water over me.

'Then they started to beat me again, but it was useless to beat a man like me who was so swollen up and looking so bad. Then they started in another way, they started to screw and break my arms and legs. And my right arm was dislocated. I felt that awful pain …They poured water on me and I came back again to life.

'Then they placed a … sort of home-made wooden thing, with a screw arrangement, on my left leg; and they started to screw so that all the flesh loosened from the bones. I felt an awful pain and fainted away again … I have still big marks here on my leg from the screw arrangement, now, four years afterwards.'

To the relief of the judges and other prosecutors, who feared delays of the Tribunal, on 7 February the French completed the presentation of their evidence. Throughout the day, the President of the Tribunal sought to prevent the repetition that had now become a common part of the trial, as much of the ground covered was now grimly familiar, one grotesque horror following another. The testimonies may have been immensely powerful, but there was simply so much documented evidence that the impact merely lay in proving the same points repeatedly. As Judge Norman Birkett was recorded as saying in the *Times* newspaper: 'The case has been proved over and over again.'

Atrocities in the East

On the morning of 8 February 1946 the Russian prosecution began its case. Like the three other Allies before him, the Soviet chief prosecutor, General Roman Andriyovych Rudenko, would deliver an opening speech that acknowledged the historical significance of the Tribunal and established that the basis of the prosecution was defined by international law rather than a desire for vengeance – even if earlier statements coming from the Soviet Union might have suggested otherwise. The Russian case was centred upon the war crimes and crimes against humanity that took place during the Nazi invasion of the East.

'I am fully conscious of the supreme historical importance of these proceedings. For the first time in the history of mankind is justice confronted with crimes committed on so vast a scale, with crimes which have entailed such grave consequences. It is for the first time that criminals who have seized an entire state and made this state an instrument of their monstrous crimes appear before a court of justice. It is also for the first time that, by judging these defendants, we sit in judgment not only on the defendants themselves, but also on the criminal institutions and organizations which they created and on the inhuman theories and ideas which they promulgated with a view to committing crimes against peace and humanity, crimes which were designed by them far in advance of their perpetration.

'... Hitlerism imposed upon the world a war which caused the freedom-loving nations innumerable privations and endless sufferings. Millions of people fell victims of the war initiated by the Hitlerite brigands who embarked on a dream of conquering the free peoples of the democratic countries and of establishing the rule of Hitlerite tyranny in Europe and in the entire world.'

Like his predecessors, Rudenko cited Kellogg–Briand, the Hague Convention and the Geneva Convention as legal precedents for the creation of the trial. He then underlined the principles of responsibility underlying the Soviets' case, but also pointed to complications that might arise.

'When several criminals conspire to commit a murder, every one of them plays a definite part. One works out the plan of murder, another waits in the car, and the third actually fires at the victim. But whatever may be the part played by any individual participant, they all are murderers and any court of law in any country will reject any attempts to assert that the first two should not be considered murderers, since they themselves had not fired the bullet.

'The more complicated and hazardous the conceived crime, the more complicated and less tangible the links connecting the individual participants. When a gang of bandits commits an assault, responsibility for the raid is also shared by those members of the gang who did not actually take part in the assault. But when the size of the gang attains extraordinary proportions, when the gang happens to be at the helm of the ship of state, when the gang commits numerous and very grave international crimes, then of course, the ties and mutual relations among the members of the gang become entangled to the utmost.'

Rudenko then launched his attack on the racial theories of Nazism:

The Soviet prosecution team with General Roman Andriyovych Rudenko (front right).

'It followed from this theory that Germans, since they belonged to the "master race", have the "right" to build their own welfare on the bones of other races and nations. This theory proclaimed that German fascist usurpers are not bound by any laws or commonly accepted rules of human morality. The "master race" is permitted to do anything. No matter how revolting and shameless, cruel, and monstrous were the actions of those individuals, they were based on the idea of the superiority of this race.

'Geography became the instrument for propagating the "preeminent importance of the Germans in the world", of their "right to dominate" other peoples. A feeling of racial superiority, arrogance, hatred, contempt, and cruelty toward other peoples was cultivated in the young.'

Here Rudenko recited the lyrics of what he described as "a German fascist song": "If all the world lies in ruins / What the devil do we care? / We still will go marching on / For today Germany belongs to us / And tomorrow the whole world."

By this time both Göring and Hess had taken off their earphones and thereafter sat in silent disdain. Indeed, Hess did not return for the afternoon session – it was reported that, not for the first time, he claimed to be suffering from a stomach complaint.

In the afternoon, the second half of Rudenko's opening focused on the impact of the war on Eastern Europe and the Soviet Union, as he began to catalogue the incomprehensible destruction wreaked by the invading Nazis. He then listed examples of prominent religious architecture – some dating back to the 11th century – that had been destroyed. Given Soviet-style communism's – at best – ambivalence towards organized religion, this was seen by some as perhaps an unusual point to be making.

'In their fierce hatred of the Soviet people and their culture, the German invaders destroyed scientific and artistic institutions, historical and cultural monuments, schools and hospitals, clubs and theaters. "No historic or artistic treasures in the East," Field

Marshal Reichenau decreed in his order, "are of importance". Side by side with the barbarous destruction and looting of villages, towns, and national cultural monuments, the Hitlerites also mocked the religious feelings of the believers among the population. They burnt, looted, destroyed, and desecrated on Soviet territory 1,670 Greek Orthodox churches, 237 Roman Catholic churches, 69 chapels, 532 synagogues, and 258 other buildings belonging to religious institutions.'

General Rudenko continued to describe the mind-boggling decimation of the state at the hands of the Nazis. These numbers were provided by the Soviet Union and, it should be said, were unverified. Indeed, there was a wide belief among the other Allies that they had been exaggerated. They nevertheless provided an effective indication of the scale of the destruction.

'The German fascist invaders completely or partially destroyed or burned 1,710 cities and more than 70,000 villages and hamlets; they burned or destroyed over 6 million buildings and rendered some 25 million persons homeless. Among the damaged cities which suffered most were the big industrial and cultural centres of Stalingrad, Sevastopol, Leningrad, Kiev, Minsk, Odessa, Smolensk, Novgorod, Pskov, Orel, Kharkov, Voronezh, Rostov-on-Don ...

'The Germano-fascist invaders destroyed 31,850 industrial establishments employing some 4 million workers ... 65,000 kilometres of railway tracks, 4,100 railway stations, 36,000 post and telegraph offices, telephone exchanges, and other installations for communications ... 40,000 hospitals and other medical institutions, 84,000 schools, technical colleges, universities, institutes for scientific research, and 43,000 public libraries.'

Rudenko was also able to offer an insight into how severely the Nazis had damaged Russia's predominantly agricultural economy:

'The Hitlerites destroyed and looted 98,000 collective farms, 1,876 state farms, and 2,890 machine and tractor stations; they slaughtered, seized or drove into Germany 7 million horses, 17 million head of horned cattle, 20 million pigs, 27 million sheep and goats, and 110 million head of poultry. The total damage caused to the Soviet Union by the criminal acts of the Hitlerite armies has been estimated at 679,000 million roubles.' [The rouble during this period was an internal currency so no exchange rates existed to indicate a value in dollars.]

In the days that followed the Soviet prosecution presented its evidence, much of which was taken from a series of 31 Extraordinary State Commission reports. Each one focused on a specific set of 'crimes' or 'atrocities' based around one area or country, including submissions from the governments of other occupied Eastern European states. As had been the case with the French prosecution, a good deal of the evidence had already been covered in documents produced by the United States prosecutors. Until, that is, the beginning of the afternoon session of 11 February 1946 – the 56th day of the trial – in which General Rudenko offered up a dramatic and unexpected prosecution witness.

The testimony of Paulus

Field Marshal Friedrich Paulus commanded Germany's 6th Army at Stalingrad. It was one of the decisive battles of the war in the East; fought from August 1942 to February 1943, it ended with the Nazi troops encircled within the city and the capture of more than a quarter of a million German military personnel. Hitler considered it Paulus's duty to take his own life rather than submit to the enemy ('here is a man who sees 50,000 or 60,000 of his soldiers die defending themselves bravely to the end; how can he surrender himself to the Bolshevists?!') and was outraged by his refusal. But Paulus, an educated man from a prominent German family, was dismissive of the Führer: 'I have no intention of shooting myself for this Bohemian corporal [Hitler's rank

Field Marshal Friedrich Paulus (centre) at Stalingrad, prior to the capture of the German 6th Army by the Soviets.

during the First World War].' Initially refusing to co-operate with his Soviet captors, he became a vocal critic of the Nazi leadership following the failed assassination attempt on Hitler in July 1944, even broadcasting his opinions on Russian radio.

Smartly dressed in a crisp blue suit, Field Marshal Paulus was escorted into the courtroom by a pair of US Army 'snowdrops'. Never once looking at the defendants, his clearly well-rehearsed responses to the prosecution ended each time with the phrase: 'To summarize, I should like to state that ... '

Paulus was first asked about his knowledge of Germany's preparations for the invasion of the Soviet Union.

> 'When I took office I found in my sphere of work, among other things, a still incomplete operational plan dealing with an attack on the Soviet Union ... it was stated that altogether about 130 to 140 German divisions would be available for this operation ... I confirm the fact that the preparation for this attack on the Soviet Union, which actually took place on 22 June 1941, dated back to the autumn of 1940.'

Paulus confirmed that the plan had been to mobilize German forces east along a front drawn between the Dnieper river in Ukraine, through Smolensk and up to Leningrad (St Petersburg) on the Baltic coast, but that it was delayed by five weeks when Hitler decided to invade Yugoslavia in April 1941. The ultimate aim was to reach the Volga–Archangel line:

> 'From a strategic point of view, the achievement of these aims would have meant the destruction of the armed forces of the Soviet Union ... the main areas of Soviet Russia with the capital, Moscow, would have been conquered and subjugated, together with the leading political and economic centre of the Soviet Union. Economically, the winning of this line would have meant the possession of important agricultural areas, the most important natural resources, including the oil wells of the Caucasus and

the main centres of production in Russia, and also the main network of communications in European Russia.'

Paulus 'summarized' that Hitler's clear aim had been 'the conquest of the Russian territories for the purpose of colonization with the utilization and spoliation of, and with the resources of which, the war in the West was to be brought to a conclusion, with the aim of finally establishing domination over Europe'.

The field marshal's final contribution to the afternoon in court was his clear and unequivocal response when General Rudenko asked him which of the defendants was an active participant in the initiation of a war of aggression against the Soviet Union.

'As far as I observed them, the top military advisers to Hitler: They are the Chief of the Supreme Command of the Armed Forces, Keitel; Chief of the Operations Branch, Jodl; and Göring, in his capacity as Reich Marshal, as Commander-in-Chief of the Air Forces and as Plenipotentiary for Armament Economy.'

In his Nuremberg Trials diary, American psychologist Gustave Gilbert recalled that the defendants were visibly shaken by Paulus's testimony. As he left the stand Göring called him a 'dirty pig' and a 'traitor' and suggested that he must have taken Soviet citizenship. (Paulus would, in fact, spend the rest of his life in communist East Germany, heading the East German Military History Research Institute.)

The following morning, Field Marshal Paulus was recalled to the witness box for questioning by the defence counsel. Without his prepared statements his responses were often monosyllabic, vague and inconclusive. Gilbert recalled Göring's reaction to Paulus's many lapses of memory; referring to Rudolf Hess's supposed mental state, he called out: 'He doesn't remember! Hess, do you know you've got a competitor?'

The main thrust of the defence counsel's questioning was that his testimony could hardly be considered impartial since he had effectively changed sides after the Battle of Stalingrad. He countered accusations that he held an official Soviet position by stating that he had been 'in a prisoner-of-war camp, like my other comrades' and that he 'was a member of a movement of German men, soldiers of all ranks and men of all classes, who had made it their aim to warn the German people at the last moment from the abyss, and to arouse them to overthrow this Hitler regime which had brought all this misery to many nations and especially to our German people'.

In the end, he made it clear that although the war of aggression against the Soviet Union constituted a 'criminal attack', his military obligation had been equally plain: 'As the situation at that time presented itself for the soldier, in connection also with the extraordinary propaganda which was put into play, I had at that time, as so many others believed, to do my duty toward my fatherland.'

Pile upon pile of corpses

After the drama of Field Marshal Paulus's appearance in court, the evidence from the prosecution once more shifted back to the Nazis' extensive self-incriminating documentation. Two days were taken up with evidence relating to the treatment of Red Army prisoners of war. Soviet prosecutor Colonel Yuri Pokrovsky read out orders that had been signed by Adolf Hitler himself:

'All clemency or humaneness towards prisoners of war is strictly condemned. A German soldier must always make his prisoner feel his superiority … Every delay in resorting to arms against a war prisoner harbours danger. The Commander-in-Chief of the Army hopes that these directions will be fully carried out.'

The prosecution drew on the testimony of Lieutenant General Ostrreich, who issued explicit orders regarding the identification of captive military personnel:

'Soviet prisoners of war are to be branded with a special and lasting mark. The brand is to consist of an acute angle of about 45 degrees with a one-centimetre length of side, pointing

Bodies piled high outside the incinerator plant at Buchenwald.

downwards on the left buttock, at about a hand's width from the rectum. This brand is to be made with the lancets available in all military units. Indian ink is to be used as colouring matter.'

As was shown earlier in the Tribunal in the case of the Nazis' forced labourers, Soviet prisoners of war were also deliberately undernourished. German High Command pointed out that since the Soviet Union had not signed up to the terms of the Geneva Convention in 1929: 'We are not obliged to supply Soviet prisoners of war with food corresponding in quantity or quality to the requirements of this regulation.' Colonel Pokrovsky listed the meagre monthly dietary provisions made for the Soviet prisoners: 'Bread, 6 kilograms; meat, 400 grams; fat, 440 grams; sugar, 600 grams.' He showed photographs of Soviet prisoners scavenging. They were 'eating the oil cakes stored for cattle food'.

Unsurprisingly, many perished. Quoting from a report on German atrocities in the Lithuanian Soviet Republic, he said:

'There was in the camp at Fort Number 6 a "hospital" for prisoners of war which in reality served as a point of transfer from the camp to the grave. The prisoners of war thrown into this "hospital" were doomed to death. According to monthly statistics of sickness among the prisoners of war in Fort Number 6, from September 1941 to July 1942, that is, over a period of 11 months only, the number of dead Soviet prisoners amounted to 13,936 … All told, 35,000 prisoners of war were buried in these graves, according to the camp documents.'

He cited a further example, that of the Stalag 350 prisoner of war camp in Riga, Latvia, where a nurse had 'repeatedly seen patients eat grass and tree leaves in order to quell the pangs of hunger'. In the same camp, it was also documented that 'the Germans tortured to death and shot over 130,000 Soviet prisoners of war'. There were many more examples offered to the courtroom.

Not for the first time at the Tribunal, the judges started to become impatient at the sheer volume of documentation being read out to the courtroom and requested that the proceedings be made as brief as possible. Yet just as those present were growing weary of the endless descriptions of horrific acts and mind-numbing statistics, on 19 February the full terror of the Nazi invasion was once again brought back into stark focus. Soviet prosecutor Lev Smirnov presented a 45-minute film entitled *The Atrocities of the German Fascist Invaders in the USSR*, which revealed the most harrowing images yet shown to the Tribunal. The film depicted the Majdanek extermination camp in occupied Poland which, uniquely, had been liberated more or less intact when the Soviets forced back the German Army from the East. Those in the courtroom were subjected to images of pile upon pile of broken and mutilated corpses, grotesque bone-crushing machines manned by other camp inmates and naked women driven towards mass graves, who were then forced to lay down before being shot. The Soviet authorities might have exaggerated the death tolls for their own ends, but this was an experience that nobody present would ever forget. And the judges made no further attempt to hurry the Soviet prosecutors.

Looting and destruction

The presentation of evidence continued as Soviet assistant prosecutor Colonel Lev Sheinin described the official Nazi policy of wholesale theft from occupied territories by using the words of Dr Robert Ley, which appeared in the Nazi newspaper *Der Angriff* in 1940: 'It is our destiny to belong to a superior race. A lower race needs less room, less clothing, less food, and less culture than a superior race.'

How this worked in practice was shown in orders issued by the operations department of the General Staff of the German Army:

'It is urgently necessary that articles of clothing be acquired by means of forced levies on the population of the occupied regions enforced by every possible means. It is necessary above all to confiscate woollen and leather gloves, coats, vests, and scarves, padded vests and trousers, leather and felt boots, and puttees.'

Other documents detailed the further seizure of property: 'Scales, sacks, grain, salt, kerosene, benzine, lamps, pots and pans, oilcloth, window blinds, curtains, rugs, phonographs, and records must be turned in to the commandant's office.'

Farms and co-operative stores were plundered by Nazi troops: 'They broke into the storehouses even when the front line was still far away. Enormous quantities of grain were stolen, including large quantities of seed.' And then when the Nazis were being repelled their actions were the same in retreat. Farms were

'plundered by retreating units ... the soldiers carried away with them butter, cheese, et cetera ... The German fascist aggressors destroyed and pillaged 98,000 collective farms, 1,876 State farms, and 2,890 machine and tractor stations. Seven million horses, 17 million head of cattle, 20 million pigs, 27 million sheep and goats, and 110 million poultry were slaughtered or shipped to Germany ... In 25 districts of the Tula region alone the invaders robbed Soviet citizens of 14,048 cows, 11,860 hogs, 28,459 sheep, 213,678 chickens, geese, and ducks, and destroyed 25,465 beehives.'

What could not be used to further the Nazi war effort was often wantonly destroyed. Houses of cultural importance, once owned by Tchaikovsky and Rimsky-Korsakov, were ransacked. Yasnaya Polyana, the estate once owned by Leo Tolstoy, was

'wrecked, profaned, and finally set on fire by the Nazi vandals. The grave of the great writer was desecrated ... Irreplaceable relics relating to the life and work of Leo Tolstoy, including rare manuscripts, books, and paintings, were either plundered by the German soldiers or thrown away and destroyed. A German officer named Schwartz, in reply to a request of one of the museum's staff collaborators to stop using the personal furniture and books of the great writer for firewood and to use wood available for this purpose, answered, 'We don't need firewood;

we shall burn everything connected with the name of your Tolstoy.'"

Murder and genocide

On 26 February 1946 – the 68th day of the trial – the charges of Crimes against Humanity were made against the Nazis and the Soviet prosecutors introduced a number of witnesses to testify. Russian peasant Jacob Grigoriev described how his village was wiped out by the invading German Army.

'On the memorable day of 28 October 1943, German soldiers suddenly raided our village and started murdering the peaceful citizens, shooting them, chasing them into the houses. On that day I was working on the threshing floor with my two sons … Suddenly a German soldier came up to us and ordered us to follow him. We were led through the village to the last house at the outskirts. There were 19 of us, all told, in that house … A little later three German machine gunners came in, accompanied by a fourth carrying a heavy revolver. We were ordered into another room … and were lined up against a wall … and they began shooting at us.'

Miraculously, he and one of his sons survived. In all, 47 villagers were massacred and every building was razed to the ground.

Another witness, Dr Eugene Kivelisha, a junior physician in the Red Army, described the 'special regime for Soviet prisoners of war in the camps'. He recounted an incident that took place during the transfer of inmates between prisoner of war camps:

'We were passing the outskirts of a little village. The peaceful civilian population came to meet us, and tried to supply us with water and bread. However, the Germans would not allow us to approach the citizens, nor would they let the population approach the column of prisoners. One of the prisoners stepped 5 or 6 meters out of the column, and without any warning was

killed by a German soldier shooting from a tommy gun. Several
of his comrades rushed to help him thinking that he was still
alive, but they too were immediately fired on without warning.
Some of them were wounded and two of them were killed.'

Prosecutor Smirnov next turned his attention to witnesses' accounts of
the treatment of the Jews in Soviet territories. Poet Abram Sutzkever
described his home city of Vilnius, Lithuania, after the Nazi invasion:

'About 80,000 Jews lived in the town. The man-hunters of the
Sonderkommandos, or as the Jews called them, the "Khapun",
broke into the Jewish houses at any time of day or night,
dragged away the men ... hardly one returned. When the Jews
found out that their kin were not coming back, a large part of
the population went into hiding. However, the Germans tracked
them with police dogs. Many were found, and any who were
averse to going with them were shot on the spot.'

After the Germans had left only 600 Jews remained – the others, over
79,000 in number, had been exterminated.

Severina Shmaglevskaya spent three years interned at Auschwitz.
Asked for proof that she had been an internee she replied: 'I have
the number which was tattooed on my arm, right here.' It was, she
confirmed, what inmates referred to as a 'visiting card'. She gave an
appalling account of the treatment of children born in or brought to the
concentration camp:

'The newborn children, if Jewish, were immediately put to
death. A few minutes after delivery the child was taken from
the mother, who never saw it again ... an order was issued that
the children were to be thrown into the crematory ovens or the
crematory ditches without previous asphyxiation with gas ...
The children were thrown in alive. Their cries could be heard
all over the camp.'

A further witness, Samuel Rajzman, described conditions at the Treblinka extermination camp, beginning with the German guards' wry description of the road that led to the gas chambers: 'It was named Himmelfahrt Street.' Prosecutor Smirnov added: 'That is to say, the "street to heaven"?' Rajzman nodded in agreement and continued.

> 'Transports arrived there every day. Their number depended on the number of trains arriving; sometimes three, four, or five trains filled exclusively with Jews … Immediately after their arrival, the people had to leave the trains in five minutes and line up on the platform. All those who were driven from the cars were divided into groups – men, children and women – all separate. They were all forced to strip immediately, and this procedure continued under the lashes of the German guards' whips. Workers who were employed in this operation immediately picked up all the clothes and carried them away to the barracks. Then the people were obliged to walk naked through the street to the gas chambers.'

He gave a horrific example of the treatment meted out to a Jewish child at Treblinka:

> 'A ten-year-old girl was brought to this building from the train with her two-year-old sister. When the elder girl saw that [the guard] Menz had taken out a revolver to shoot her two-year-old sister, she threw herself upon him, crying out, and asking why he wanted to kill her. He did not kill the little sister; he threw her alive into the oven and then killed the elder sister.'

Rajzman gave a further example of the sadism of *Scharführer* (squad leader) Menz when an aged woman and her pregnant daughter were brought to what was known as the '*Lazarett*' – a fake medical building that displayed a Red Cross flag:

'When the child was born, Menz asked the grandmother – that is, the mother of this woman – whom she preferred to see killed first. The grandmother begged to be killed. But, of course, they did the opposite; the newborn baby was killed first, then the child's mother, and finally the grandmother.'

After the war, Willi Menz returned to his former job as a milkman. In 1965 he finally faced justice when charged with complicity in the mass murder of 700,000 Jews at Treblinka. He received a life sentence.

The prosecution case against the major war criminals finally ended on 6 March 1946 – 75 days after Robert H. Jackson had made his impassioned opening statement. In all, 33 witnesses had been called to give testimony, some of whom had a significant impact on the proceedings. Through the power of the moving image, though, it was the supporting films that perhaps made the most dramatic and lasting impression on those in the courtroom. In the end, though, the most incriminating evidence came from the Nazis themselves, in the form of the careful and voluminous documentation of their own modus operandi – from the very beginnings of National Socialism to the eventual collapse of Nazi Germany.

CHAPTER 8

The Case for the Defence

Three days before the Nazi defendants were due to begin their testimonies, a speech of historic significance took place almost five thousand miles across the Atlantic, in the unlikely location of Fulton, Missouri. Britain's wartime leader, Sir Winston Churchill, had found himself ignominiously voted out of power when the Labour Party received a landslide victory in the 1945 General Election and yet even as Leader of the Opposition he was able to use his undoubted oratorical skills to cause disquiet across the globe. On 5 March 1946, introduced by President Harry Truman, Churchill gave a lecture at Fulton's Westminster College in which he identified what he saw as the greatest new threat facing Western civilization:

'Nobody knows what Soviet Russia and its Communist international organization intends to do in the immediate future. Or what are the limits, if any, to their expansive and proselytizing tendencies ... From Stettin in the Baltic to Trieste in the Adriatic, an "iron curtain" has descended across the Continent. Behind that line lie all the capitals of the ancient states of Central and Eastern Europe. Warsaw, Berlin, Prague, Vienna, Budapest, Belgrade, Bucharest and Sofia, all these famous cities and the populations around them lie in what I must call the Soviet sphere, and all are subject in one form or another, not only to Soviet influence but to a very high and, in many cases, increasing measure of control from Moscow.'

Speaking at Fulton, Missouri on 5 March 1946, Britain's wartime leader Winston Churchill first uttered the famous 'Iron Curtain' phrase.

It was not the first time the phrase 'iron curtain' had been used to describe the ideological divide between the communist East and the capitalist West. Joseph Goebbels had already employed it in *Das Reich* in February 1945: 'Over all this territory … an iron curtain would at once descend.' Yet for some historians Churchill's 'Sinews of Peace' speech – as it is widely known – quite literally defined the starting point of the Cold War.

The implications of the speech were not lost on the defendants at Nuremberg. The two great enemies of National Socialism were the Jews and the communist Bolsheviks. In Albert Speer's diaries from Spandau Prison in West Berlin, he recalled the 'tremendous excitement' at Churchill's speech and how Hess had declared that: 'History will not be deceived. The Führer and I always prophesied it. This coalition had to break up sooner or later.'

The relationship between the Soviet Union and the other Allied powers certainly hardened at the end of the war, but Churchill's speech presaged a new level of hostility, a great ideological divide between East and West that would cast a giant shadow over world politics for the next 45 years. Yet if Göring, Hess, Keitel and their colleagues thought it likely to signal a change in their personal fortunes they were mistaken.

Confidence among the defence counsel was, nevertheless, higher than it had been since the beginning of the trial. Fears of a Soviet-style fait accompli show trial, with the accused prejudged and already sentenced to death, had abated. In spite of Göring's frequent posturing and harrumphing from the defendants' box, the Nuremberg Trial seemed more impartial than they might have expected. It was also clear from the prosecution presentations that the individual cases against the defendants were not all equally strong, and that some were more culpable than others. If a uniform sentence were to be handed down it would surely suggest a lack of subtlety on the part of the judges, not to mention the fact that they would be pandering to the view held in some quarters – including by a number of the defendants themselves – that Nuremberg was a waste of everybody's time, and all of the defendants should simply have been executed. That would have been the end of the matter.

Göring's defence

The atmosphere of anticipation that had greeted the opening of the Nuremberg Trials nearly three months earlier had abated within days. This might have been a unique event – unprecedented in the appallingness of the horrors depicted – but there was too much repetition and legal 'process' to maintain that initial interest. This changed on the morning of Friday, 8 March 1946 with the opening for the defence, which was to begin with the most infamous Nazi on trial, Hermann Göring. Until all but the latter stages of the war, Göring had been Adolf Hitler's de facto Number Two, so the charge brought against him was that he played a central role in all four indictments. The prosecution case against Göring looked watertight.

As early as 4 February, Hermann Göring's defence counsel, Dr Otto Stahmer, had requested a three-week adjournment after the conclusion of the prosecution to enable them to properly prepare their cases. While the prosecutors were amenable to the idea, the judges were adamant 'that the Tribunal, which is directed by the Charter [of London] to secure an expeditious hearing of the issues raised by the charges, will not permit any delay either in the preparation of the defense or of the Trial'.

Dr Stahmer launched Göring's defence by calling as a witness General Karl Bodenschatz, formerly the liaison officer between Göring, in his role as commander-in-chief of the Luftwaffe, and Hitler's headquarters. When asked if Göring knew about the attacks on the Jews on Kristallnacht (9–10 November 1938), Bodenschatz read his unconvincing response from a prepared statement:

'Göring had no previous knowledge of these incidents. I inferred that from his demeanour … When he heard of these happenings he was dismayed and condemned them. A few days later he went with proof to the Führer and complained about the people who had instigated these incidents … He was violently opposed to these individual acts of barbarism. He criticized them severely as unjust, as economically unreasonable and harmful to our prestige in foreign countries.'

Contrary to the picture that had been painted earlier in the Tribunal, Göring was a man who

> 'worked decisively for the preservation of peace ... In his feelings, thoughts, and actions, as far as human society was concerned, he was a benefactor to all in need. He was always ready to help those who were in need, for instance sick people, wounded, the relatives of those who had been killed in the war and of prisoners of war.'

Robert Jackson's cross-examination was nothing less than brutal. With his script now gone, Bodenschatz's testimony was demolished as he struggled and sweated his way through an afternoon of inconsistent responses to incriminating questions. He was followed to the stand by Secretary of State for the Air Ministry Erhard Milch. If anything, Milch was even more ineffectual as a witness. He reiterated the idea of Göring 'the man of peace' ('in my opinion, he was against war') before discussing the concentration camps. Milch claimed to have been only aware of Dachau and one other camp. The conditions for internees ('volunteers') were, he claimed:

> 'clean and properly organized ... They had their own slaughterhouse and their own bakery. We insisted on having the food of the internees served to us. The food was good and one of the camp leaders explained that they fed the inmates very well as they were engaged on heavy work.'

Under cross-examination from Robert Jackson, his testimony was easily unravelled. Records showed that Milch had attended a Central Planning Board meeting in which Sauckel had reported: 'Out of the 5 million foreign workers who arrived in Germany, not even 200,000 came voluntarily.'

British prosecutor G.D. Roberts continued to probe the witness, who claimed to know nothing about plans for military aggression nor air pressure experiments on prisoners from Dachau – in spite of a letter from

Himmler: 'Dear Milch ... both high pressure and cold water experiments have been carried out ... '

Milch left the stand a discredited witness. He would later be tried and convicted at one of the 'subsequent' Nuremberg Trials.

A more impressive witness came in the form of Field Marshal Albert Kesselring. Resplendent in his smart Luftwaffe uniform, Kesselring gave clear and direct answers to Dr Stahmer about his role in the air attacks on Poland in 1939 and the way in which they were conducted: 'I can assert that everything that was humanly possible was done to hit military targets only and to spare civilian targets.' And he maintained that Göring's evacuation of the art treasures from the Monte Cassino monastery in Italy came under the heading of 'preventive measures', because the Nazis were 'having these places cleared if they were liable to air raids'.

Unruffled by Robert Jackson's cross-examination, it was only when British prosecutor Sir David Maxwell Fyfe took over the questioning that his testimony faltered. He provided evidence that he had ordered the devastating bombing raid on Rotterdam at 1.30 p.m. on 14 May 1940, even though negotiations for surrender had begun earlier in the day.

Maxwell Fyfe then turned to Kesselring's role in the Italian campaign, showing evidence of his orders for the brutal treatment of captives and partisans:

'It is the duty of all troops and police in my command to adopt the severest measures ... Wherever there is evidence of considerable numbers of partisan groups, a proportion of the male population of the area will be arrested; and in the event of an act of violence being committed, these men will be shot.'

He then read from a document detailing events that took place nine days after Kesselring's orders had been given:

'Two German soldiers were killed and a third wounded in a fight with partisans in the village of Civitella. Fearing reprisals, the inhabitants evacuated the village, but when the Germans discovered this, punitive action was postponed. On June 29, when the local inhabitants were returned and when feeling secure once more, the Germans carried out a well-organized reprisal ... Innocent inhabitants were often shot on sight. During that day 212 men, women, and children in the immediate district were killed. Some of the dead women were found completely naked ... Ages of the dead ranged from 1 year to 84 years. Approximately one hundred houses were destroyed by fire. Some of the victims were burned alive in their homes.'

'That is the report of the United Nations War Crimes Commission on the incident,' Maxwell Fyfe declared. 'Now, Witness, do you really think that military necessity commands the killing of babies of one and people of 84?'

'No,' came Kesselring's reply. (Field Marshal Kesselring was later tried by a British military tribunal in Venice in 1947 and sentenced to death for the execution of Italian hostages and incitement to kill Italian civilians. Since the death penalty was seen in Italy as a relic of the time of Mussolini, his sentence was commuted and he was released in 1954.)

Göring takes the stand

In truth, Göring's witnesses had been a disaster, their testimonies picked apart with ease. On 13 March 1946 – the 80th day of the trial – Reichsmarschall Hermann Göring himself came to the stand. His lawyer, Dr Stahmer, began by asking him for a short account of his life. During the First World War, Göring had been a flying ace who eventually headed Jagdgeschwader 1, the 'Flying Circus' of Manfred von Richthofen, the famous Red Baron. He joined the Nazis in 1922 after hearing a speech by Hitler and quickly became one of the most influential figures of National Socialism. Göring was a clever, quick-witted man. Although widely caricatured by the Allies during the war as a fat, grinning, over-indulgent drug addict, incarceration had been positive for Göring's health. Prison rations and exercise had seen his weight drop dramatically and his fitness rise and he had been weaned off his drug dependencies. He gave a self-assured performance, reading largely from a script prepared with his lawyer.

Göring knew that as far as the Tribunal was concerned his was a lost cause. He fully expected to receive the death sentence and it was clear he intended to go down fighting. So he did not hesitate to boast of his relationship with the Führer and his role in the Nazi Party, the Luftwaffe and Hitler's cabinet. He was proud of the part he had played in the creation of the Reich:

> 'In the Reich there was a majority based on one thing; in Prussia, on another; in Bavaria, on yet another; and in Hesse, on something quite different. It was impossible in this manner to establish Reich sovereignty and a Reich which could be great again. Therefore, I suggested to the Führer that the state parliaments should be dissolved and done away with as a matter of principle.'

He was clear in discussing the rationale for the Nazi attitude against the Jews:

> 'Everywhere Jewry was in the lead in the fight against National Socialism, whether in the press, in politics, in cultural life by making National Socialism contemptible and ridiculous, or in the economic sphere. Whoever was a National Socialist could not get a position; the National Socialist businessman could not get supplies or space for advertisements, and so on. All this naturally resulted in a strong defensive attitude on the part of the Party and led from the very beginning to an intensification of the fight, such as had not originally been the intention of the program. For the program aimed very definitely at one thing above all – that Germany should be led by Germans.'

Göring referred to the concentration camps as

> 'protective custody ... whether or not one could prove that these people were involved in a traitorous act or an act hostile to the

Nazi leader Hermann Göring faces the prosecutors at Nuremberg.

State, whether or not one could expect such an act from them, such an act must be prevented and the possibility eliminated by means of protective custody.'

And he claimed to have no knowledge of what went on in the camps after Himmler and the SS took over. (He was particularly scornful of Himmler, whose motives he described as 'less of a political and more of a confused mystical nature'.)

As far as Germany's use of Soviet resources following the invasion was concerned, he argued that this was quite legitimate: 'If one then gains possession of that economy, it is to one's interest to carry out this economy only insofar, of course, as the interests of one's own war needs are concerned – that goes without saying.'

In any case, he maintained this was nothing compared with the Soviet Union's activities in what soon would become East Germany:

'Our making claims on the Russian state economy for German purposes, after the conquest of those territories, was just as natural and just ... as it was for Russia when she occupied German territories, but with this difference, that we did not dismantle and transport away the entire Russian economy down to the last bolt and screw, as is being done here. These are measures which result from the conduct of war. I naturally take complete responsibility for them.'

In defending Germany against the charges that it had violated international agreements, Göring quoted an unlikely source:

'The regulations on land warfare of the Hague Convention are in my opinion not an instrument which can be used as a basis for a modern war, because they do not take into consideration the essential principles of this war; the war in the air, the economic war, and the war of propaganda ... I should like to say the same words which one of our greatest, most important, and toughest opponents, the British Prime Minister, Winston

Churchill, used: "In the struggle for life and death there is in the end no legality."'

When asked if the Nazi Party programme was ever achieved by illegal means, his response was worthy of the wiliest of politicians:

'Of course, they were to be achieved by every means. The conception "illegal" should perhaps be clarified. If I aim at a revolution, then it is an illegal action for the state then in existence. If I am successful, then it becomes a fact and thereby legal and law.'

If there was a central theme of the three days in which Göring talked, almost uninterrupted, at the stand it was not only of personal responsibility, but pride in that responsibility. When discussing the enactment of laws against the Jews:

'Although I received oral and written orders and commands from the Führer to issue and carry out these laws, I assume full and absolute responsibility for these laws which bear my signature; for I issued them and consequently am responsible, and do not propose to hide in any way behind the Führer order.'

And he extended this train of thought when discussing the 'Leadership Principle' (*Führerprinzip*), refuting the notion that it removed responsibility and obligation from the individual:

'I upheld this principle and I still uphold it positively and consciously. One must not make the mistake of forgetting that the political structure in different countries has different origins, different developments. Something which suits one country extremely well would perhaps fail completely in another. Germany, through the long centuries of monarchy, has always had a leadership principle.'

He argued that democracy had arrived in Germany at a time when the state had reached 'rock-bottom'. There was, he explained, a total lack of unity caused by the number of parties and

> 'continuous unrest caused by elections ... Authority lay with the masses and responsibility was with the leader, instead of the other way about. I am of the opinion that for Germany – particularly at that moment of its lowest ebb, when it was necessary for all forces to be welded together in a positive fashion – the Leadership Principle – that is, authority from above downwards and responsibility from below upwards – was the only possibility.'

It was without doubt a tour de force that left Göring exhausted. Heavily reported by the press, the *Daily Express* described it as the 'last-ditch stand of the Nazi regime'.

'Damage limitation'

Having had the weekend to recuperate, Göring returned to court on Monday, 18 March 1946 to face his cross-examination. It began with questions and requests for clarification from the defence counsel representing either co-defendants or organizations such as the SS. Most of this could be categorized as 'damage limitation'. Mid-morning, however, Robert Jackson rose to begin the cross-examination for the prosecution. Any hopes of a dazzling opening were soon to be dashed as Jackson fired off question after question about those policies of the Nazi Party that had enabled them to gain power. His interest, of course, was in proving the case for conspiracy and his line of questioning was an attempt to show that the crimes had been fundamental to the origins of the Nationalsozialistische Deutsche Arbeiterpartei. Yet while Jackson offered a series of 'yes' or 'no' questions, Göring refused to play ball, providing each question with a lengthy and detailed reply, at which Jackson grew increasingly agitated.

Jackson attempted to pin some of the blame on Göring for the Reichstag fire of 27 February 1933 and the murder of SA Chief of Staff

Ernst Röhm, but he had no conclusive proof. Göring said the accusation that he had provided materials for the fire had come from the foreign press and that: 'I had no reason or motive for setting fire to the Reichstag. From the artistic point of view I did not at all regret that the assembly chamber was burned; I hoped to build a better one.'

His only regret was that the Kroll Opera House was then used as a meeting place by the German parliament, since 'the opera seemed to me much more important than the Reichstag'. He went on to refer to a joke he'd once made. Dressed as Nero 'in a red toga and holding a lyre in my hand, I looked on at the fire and played while the Reichstag was burning'.

The following day Göring left the stand briefly to enable another defence witness to give testimony. Swedish businessman Birger Dahlerus had visited Göring in August 1939 in an attempt to broker peace and had written about his efforts in a book called *The Last Attempt*. By calling Dahlerus to the stand, the defence team aimed to show once again how Göring had attempted to persuade Hitler to avoid war with Britain. Yet only minutes after beginning his cross-examination, Sir David Maxwell Fyfe had to all intents and purposes turned Dahlerus into a prosecution witness. One example from the book cited a conversation with Göring in which he 'made clear that he would demand the return of Danzig and certain rights over the Polish Corridor [a narrow strip of land between East Prussia and the German mainland that enabled Poland to access the Baltic Sea]'.

Even though Göring was cast in a negative light and was angered by Dahlerus's book, he remained irrepressible when Robert Jackson continued his cross-examination. The two quibbled about his having taken part in a meeting of the Counsel for the Defence of the Reich and then Jackson produced a 1935 document in which Göring was purported to have planned the 'liberation of the Rhine', at that time a demilitarized zone. Göring pointed out to him that the document was 'preparation for the clearing of the Rhine. It is a purely technical preparation that has nothing at all to do with the liberation of the Rhineland.'

To Jackson's embarrassment, this document was not about plans for the military liberation of the Rhineland region but concerned the removal of obstacles, such as 'freighters, tugboats' from the River Rhine should sudden mobilization become necessary. Secret military planning, Göring pointed out, was quite legitimate: 'I do not think I can recall reading beforehand the publication of the mobilization preparations of the United States.'

This was the point at which Jackson lost his temper:

'I respectfully submit to the Tribunal that this witness is not being responsive, and has not been in his examination ... It is perfectly futile to spend our time if we cannot have responsive answers to our questions ... I respectfully submit ... that he be required to answer my questions and reserve his explanations for his counsel to bring out.'

Tribunal President Sir Geoffrey Lawrence defused the row quickly: 'Perhaps we had better adjourn now at this stage.'

As the day in court ended, the confident and authoritative Göring had once again shown himself to be a formidable figure in court; Jackson, for all his skills as an orator, received widespread criticism for such an ineffective cross-examination.

'Wilted and bedraggled'

On the third day of Jackson's cross-examination, he began with a complaint to the Tribunal about the latitude being given to the defendant and sought to prevent the trial turning into a 'bickering contest between counsel and witness ... I am now moving that this witness be instructed that he must answer my questions "yes" or "no".'

Lawrence agreed but nevertheless insisted that 'he may make such explanations as may be necessary after answering questions directly in that way, and that such explanations must be brief and not be speeches'. Although some of Göring's replies had been long-winded, they fell within the Tribunal's framework. Jackson reluctantly agreed to 'bow to the ruling', but he was visibly disgruntled and it continued to have an effect on his performance in court.

Jackson was more successful when he was able to deploy

documentary evidence against Göring. He chipped away at the image the defendant had managed to create of an urbane, cultured man, by highlighting crude, anti-Semitic remarks. It began with a conversation between Göring and Dr Goebbels that Jews should only be allowed to sit down on trains

> 'after all Germans have secured seats. They must not mix with the Germans; if there is no more room, they will have to stand in the corridor ... I would give the Jews one coach or one compartment, and should ... the train be overcrowded ... he will be kicked out ... and will have to sit alone in the toilet all the way.'

With regard to holiday resorts:

> 'We will give the Jews a certain part of the forest, and Alpers will see to it that the various animals, which are damnably like the Jews – the Elk too has a hooked nose – go into the Jewish enclosure and settle down among them.'

More than a little rattled, Göring now faced evidence of his role in the Holocaust. Jackson read out a letter from him to Himmler and Heydrich: 'I hereby charge you with making all necessary preparations in regard to organizational and financial matters for bringing about a complete solution of the Jewish question in the German sphere of influence in Europe.'

Göring attempted to claim that mistranslations had taken place – it should have read 'total solution' rather than 'final [or "complete"] solution' – but its meaning was clear to the court.

Neither was he able to brush off how looted Jewish art had found its way into his possession. Jackson read from a letter written by art historian Dr Hermann Bunjes:

> 'With me as his guide, the Reich Marshal inspected the exhibited art treasures and made a selection of those works of art which

were to go to the Führer, and those which were to be placed in his own collection."

Göring claimed, unconvincingly, that he had paid for any additions to his private collection.

Jackson, though, concluded his cross-examination on another sour note. Turning to the bombing of Warsaw, he attempted to demonstrate the intention by the Luftwaffe to bomb the house of the American ambassador. He showed the defendant what purported to be aerial photographs of the target. However, as a decorated pilot and founder of the Luftwaffe, this was a subject about which Göring had considerable knowledge. The photographs were, he argued, 'taken from an oblique angle, as though they had been taken from a church steeple rather than from an airplane, from which generally only vertical pictures are taken because of the built-in camera'.

Göring's confidence was high at this point: 'None of these pictures give any proof that they were taken by the Luftwaffe. However, let us assume that they were taken by the Luftwaffe, so that further questions will be facilitated.'

Demolished by superior technical knowledge, there was nowhere for Jackson to go with this point. Once again it would be left to Maxwell Fyfe, the cunning trial lawyer, to bring down the prize defendant. Over the course of two days he dealt Göring the heaviest blows he would receive. Focusing on the Stalag Luft III murders – where a prison break resulted in the execution of 50 recaptured prisoners of war (and on which the film *The Great Escape* had loosely been based) – he sought to prove Göring's central involvement. He quickly dismantled Göring's claim that he had been on leave when the executions had taken place and on 21 March he launched a relentless attack. He read documents from Field Marshal Milch and Lieutenant General Grosch:

'There was a decision by the Führer to the effect that, on recapture, the escaped British airmen were not to be handed back to the Luftwaffe but were to be shot ... The circle of those in the know was to be kept as small as possible.'

He went on to say that High Command 'had told them that the Reich Marshal was informed'.

'What I am suggesting,' Maxwell Fyfe snapped, 'is that both you and Field Marshal Milch are saying you knew nothing about it, when you did, and are leaving the responsibility on the shoulders of your junior officers.'

Shaken and blustering, Göring was unable to give a convincing response. Nor was he able to refute that he had prior knowledge of the invasion of Poland, the attacks on neutral Belgium and Holland, forced labour at Auschwitz or atrocities committed against partisans.

The general consensus at Nuremberg was that – Robert Jackson's dreadful performance notwithstanding – the prosecution's cross-examination of Hermann Göring had been a success. His preening pomp had dominated the first half of his defence, but by the time of its conclusion on 22 March the *New York Times* reported him as 'wilted and bedraggled'. In his memoirs, Maxwell Fyfe (under his title Lord Kilmuir), would describe Göring as the 'most formidable witness' he had ever cross-examined.

Rudolf Hess

Throughout the trial there had been concerns about the mental state of Rudolf Hess. Before the Tribunal began, chief psychologist Douglas Kelley diagnosed his condition as 'a true psychoneurosis, primarily of the hysterical type, engrafted on a basic paranoid and schizoid personality, with amnesia, partly genuine and partly feigned'. But he confirmed that he was fit to stand trial. Yet throughout the first three months Hess had cut an extremely awkward figure in the defendants' box. Seemingly in a world of his own, he was prone to sudden dramatic movements and gestures. Nobody knew for certain how much of this was the act of a faker but he certainly gave the appearance of a deeply troubled man.

At the end of the afternoon of 22 March 1946, Hess's defence counsel, Dr Alfred Seidl, declared to the Tribunal that Hess would not give testimony himself:

'Before commencing the submission of evidence I have to make the following remarks ... The Defendant Hess contests

A deeply troubled Rudolf Hess is pictured in his cell at Nuremberg.

the jurisdiction of the Tribunal where other than war crimes proper are the subject of the Trial. However, he specifically assumes full responsibility for all laws or decrees which he has signed.'

Since Hess had been a British prisoner of war since his abortive peace mission to Scotland in 1941, Seidl argued that there was little with which he could be charged under the third and fourth indictments (war crimes and crimes against humanity), and that the second indictment (crimes against peace) was not punishable under international law. Lawrence was clear that there could be no challenge to the jurisdiction of the Tribunal under the terms of the Charter of London, and that it cared little for the defendant's approval one way or the other. (In fact, according to the diary of psychologist Gilbert, it was less his refusal to recognize the court than that both Göring and Seidl had 'urged him not to take the stand'.

Hess had never denied his role in the Nazi Party nor his close relationship with the Führer – Hitler had even dictated *Mein Kampf* to him from his prison cell and Hess had acted as his editor. As the de facto third-in-command, he held great influence over Nazi policy in the 1930s and he was a signatory to the anti-Semitic Nuremberg Laws. But Dr Seidl emphasized that Hess's mission to Scotland had been solely to secure peace. He produced an affidavit from Hess's long-term personal secretary Hildegard Fath, who recalled the contents of the letter that he left for Hitler before taking his flight: 'From the content of the letter the definite impression was to be gained that Hess undertook this extraordinary flight in order to prevent further bloodshed, and in order to create favourable conditions for the conclusion of a peace.'

She also disputed the idea that Hess had played some part in the treatment of the Jews in Poland: 'Such a proposal would be totally contradictory to the behaviour and attitude which the Führer's Deputy displayed with regard to similar questions on other occasions.'

Since Hess was not present there was no cross-examination by the prosecution. The case took barely a day to conclude.

Joachim von Ribbentrop

The case against Germany's former foreign minister (and previously ambassador to the United Kingdom) was extremely strong on all four counts. Here was another figure who was implicated almost by virtue of his high position within the Nazi Party and his close relationship with Adolf Hitler. In captivity, however, he proved to be a somewhat pathetic figure, reviled by many of his co-defendants.

The defence of Ribbentrop began on 26 March 1946 with an announcement from his counsel, Dr Martin Horn: 'This morning the doctor told me that Ribbentrop is suffering from so-called vasomotor disturbances in his speech.'

A short while later, American chief prosecutor Thomas Dodd would introduce some information of his own:

'I have talked with Colonel Andrus and with one of the Army doctors in attendance ... our understanding is that Ribbentrop is not ill and is able to take the witness stand; that he is nervous, and appears to be frightened, but he is not disabled in any sense and is capable of testifying.'

The day nevertheless went ahead without Ribbentrop, Horn instead offering a chaotic selection of documents, more than half of which would be deemed inadmissible. He also produced a witness, Baron Gustav Steengracht von Moyland, who had been Ribbentrop's adjutant before being promoted to State Secretary at the Foreign Ministry. The main purpose of Steengracht's testimony had been to show that Ribbentrop had exerted little influence over Hitler:

'The foreign policy, not only on its basic lines, but also usually down to the most minute details, was determined by Hitler himself. Ribbentrop frequently stated that the Führer needed no Foreign Minister, he simply wanted a foreign political secretary. Ribbentrop, in my opinion, would have been satisfied with such a position because then at least, backed by Hitler's authority, he could have eliminated partly the destructive and indirect foreign political influences and their sway on Hitler. Perhaps he might then have had a chance of influencing Hitler's speeches.'

He reinforced this point when addressing the treatment of the Church and the Jews: 'I know that Ribbentrop spoke frequently with Hitler on this theme ... But he explained to me again and again when he returned from Hitler: "Hitler cannot be spoken to on this point."'

He may not have been able to influence official policy, but Horn pressed the case that Ribbentrop was able to restrain some of Hitler's excesses, such as preventing the retaliatory executions of 10,000 prisoners of war following the RAF bombing of Dresden:

'On a suggestion by Goebbels, the Führer intended, as reprisal for the holocaust of Dresden, to have English and American prisoners of war – I believe mostly airmen – shot. I went immediately to Ribbentrop and informed him of this. [He] became very excited; he turned pale as death ... Then Ribbentrop got up immediately and went to Hitler, came back, I think after half an hour, and told me that he had succeeded in having Hitler withdraw this order.'

Dr Horn called two further defence witnesses. His former secretary Margarete Blank undermined the previous witness by painting a picture of a weak figure who was thoroughly in thrall to his leader:

'As far as I can judge Herr von Ribbentrop always showed the greatest admiration and veneration for Adolf Hitler. To enjoy the Führer's confidence, to justify it by his conduct and work was his chief aim, to which he devoted all his efforts ... In cases of differences of opinion between himself and the Führer, Herr von Ribbentrop subordinated his own opinion ... Once a decision had been made by Adolf Hitler there was no more criticism afterwards.'

Nazi Foreign Minister Joachim von Ribbentrop was an anglophile who liked to wear a top hat when he was in London. This photograph was taken in 1938.

She told the court that he would then present Hitler's views to his subordinates as if they were his own: 'If the Führer expressed his will, it was always equivalent to a military order.'

The final witness was Foreign Ministry interpreter Dr Paul Schmidt, whose testimony proved to be a gift for the prosecution. Offering little in the way of defence for Ribbentrop, under cross-examination from Maxwell Fyfe he confirmed official foreign policy:

'The general objectives of the Nazi leadership were apparent from the start, namely, the domination of the European Continent, to be achieved, first, by the incorporation of all German-speaking groups in the Reich, and secondly, by territorial expansion under the slogan of *"Lebensraum"*.'

Ribbentrop finally took the stand on the afternoon of 28 March. Pallid and withdrawn, Hitler's former foreign minister looked defeated before he even began his testimony, which was a lacklustre piece delivered in a lifeless tone. He described his early career and talked of 'the severe stipulations of Versailles' and 'the denial of equality' and how 'the natural will of the German people broke through to resist this treatment'.

Initially Ribbentrop was unconvinced by the National Socialists:

'Friends of mine spoke to me about Adolf Hitler, whom I did not know at the time, they asked me, "What sort of a man is Adolf Hitler? What will come of it? What is it?" I said to them frankly at that time, "Give Germany a chance and you will not have Adolf Hitler. Do not give her a chance, and Adolf Hitler will come into power." That was approximately in 1930 or 1931. Germany was not given the chance, so on 30 January 1933 he came – the National Socialists seized power.'

His view changed following his first personal encounter in 1932: 'I left that meeting with Hitler convinced that this man, if anyone, could save Germany from these great difficulties and that distress which existed at the time.'

Ribbentrop's rambling testimony continued the following day, earning him a rebuke from Lawrence, who considered the history of the Nazi Party and the injustices of Versailles to have been covered in full. Dr Horn also received a rebuke from the President: 'It is the duty of counsel to examine their witnesses and not to leave them simply to make speeches.'

In truth, the charges against Ribbentrop were already looking seamless before Maxwell Fyfe began another brutally effective cross-examination, uncovering lie after lie with documentary evidence of Ribbentrop's own words. He cited a quote from Italy's foreign minister, Count Ciano, who had asked Ribbentrop, shortly before the invasion of Poland: 'What do you want, the Corridor or Danzig?' Ribbentrop replied that Germany was no longer interested: 'We want war.'

He had also evidently told Count Ciano

'that he did not believe that England and France would assist Poland without further questions, but that at all times he had reckoned with the possibility of intervention by the Western Powers. He was glad now about the course of events, because, first of all, it had always been clear that the clash would have to come sooner or later and that it was inevitable.'

Maxwell Fyfe ridiculed him when he dismissed this as 'diplomatic talk'.

'Don't you think there is any requirement to tell the truth in a political conversation?'

And there were some curious lines of questioning. He asked Ribbentrop how many houses he owned as foreign minister. He replied that he had six houses. Maxwell Fyfe asked him to look at a map on which red spots marked concentration camps. 'We will see now one of the reasons for the location of your various residences,' he told the defendant, pointing out the close proximity of one of the houses to a particular red spot. Ribbentrop claimed to know of only two concentration camps before the Nuremberg Trial.

Maxwell Fyfe was incredulous: 'Are you telling the Tribunal that anyone could be a responsible minister in that country where these hundreds of concentration camps existed and not know anything about them except two?'

'It may be amazing,' Ribbentrop replied, 'but it is one hundred per cent true.'

'I suggest to you,' came the retort, 'that it is not only amazing, but that it is so incredible that it must be false.'

The lies continued. Maxwell Fyfe showed Ribbentrop an application to join the *Totenkopf*, the Death's Head Division of the SS, but Ribbentrop denied it.

'Don't you remember getting a special Death's-Head ring and dagger from Himmler for your services?' Maxwell Fyfe asked.

Again, the defendant denied it. Maxwell Fyfe then produced a letter to the Personnel Office of the Reichsführer SS, confirming that Ribbentrop's ring size was 17.

On the final day of Ribbentrop's defence case the French prosecutor, Edgar Faure, gave a final twist of the dagger when he referred to an earlier testimony from witness Paul Schmidt regarding a meeting between Hitler and Hungarian Regent Miklós Horthy, in which he noted that: 'The Foreign Minister [Ribbentrop] declared that the Jews were either to be exterminated or sent to concentration camps. There was no other solution.'

'It appears from this document that you thought there were concentration camps in Hungary,' Faure continued, 'and yet you said yesterday that you did not know there were any in Germany.'

Wilhelm Keitel

Chief of Staff of the High Command from 1938 to 1945, Field Marshal Wilhelm Keitel may not have been well known to the public outside Germany but within Nuremberg he was nonetheless regarded as one of the most significant defendants. His counsel, Dr Otto Nelte, a former industrial lawyer from Siegburg, began his defence by asking him to describe his military career.

'I was a soldier by inclination and conviction. For more than 44 years without interruption I served my country and my people as a soldier, and I tried to do my best in the service of my profession.'

This would be central to his defence, that as a military man his obligation was to obey commands.

'I believed that I should do this as a matter of duty, labouring unceasingly and giving myself completely to those tasks which fell to me in my many and diverse positions.'

And this was his role regardless of whom he was serving.

'I did this with the same devotion under the Kaiser, under President Ebert [of the Weimar Republic], under Field Marshal von Hindenburg, and under the Führer, Adolf Hitler.'

When faced with the accusation that he had participated in the planning and preparation of wars of aggression, he responded with the view that the term was meaningless. He was, he declared,

'a purely political concept and not a military one ... The Wehrmacht and the soldier are a tool of the politicians, they are not qualified in my opinion to decide or to judge whether these military operations did or did not constitute a war of aggression ... Military officers should not have authority to decide this question ... These decisions are not the task of the soldier, but solely that of the statesman.'

Throughout his examination, Keitel's answers remained admirably consistent, his central theme being that politicians made the decisions and the military enacted those decisions without question. As logical as this may have seemed, however, it ignored the fact, laid out at the beginning of the trial, that soldiers were still subject to international law.

Keitel was widely regarded in government circles as one of Hitler's most fervent and obedient 'yes' men, and was privately referred to as 'Lackeitel' – a play on the German word '*Lakei*' ('lackey'). In his view, he was not truly responsible for the myriad incriminating orders bearing his signature because they were Hitler's orders. As a military man, he was merely facilitating them.

'The traditional training and concept of duty of the German officers, which taught unquestioning obedience to superiors who bore responsibility, led to an attitude – regrettable in retrospect – which caused them to shrink from rebelling against these orders and these methods even when they recognized their illegality and inwardly refuted them.'

Nevertheless, in that response could be found a degree of recognition that crimes had been committed. 'The Führer, Hitler, abused his authority,' he continued, 'in an irresponsible way with respect to us.'

It was Russia's prosecutor, General Rudenko, who first took on the cross-examination of Keitel. He established that Hitler held only the barest of military qualifications when compared to the professional soldier Keitel, and so surely, he asked, 'With your thorough military training and great experience, [you] could have had an opportunity of influencing Hitler, very considerably, in solving questions of a strategic and military nature, as well as other matters pertaining to the Armed Forces?'

Keitel maintained that this was most definitely untrue. He painted a picture of Hitler as an autodidact who had studied in private and 'acquired his vast knowledge by himself … Only a genius can do that', he declared. Once again, he sought to minimize his own influence: 'I must admit openly that I was the pupil and not the master.'

Keitel had certainly seemed to be doomed by evidence, having signed the infamous *Nacht und Nebel* ('Night and Fog') decree that sought to intimidate local populations into submission and ultimately resulted in the deaths of thousands of resistance fighters. 'Efficient and enduring intimidation can only be achieved either by capital punishment or by measures by which the relatives of the criminals do not know the fate of the criminal,' ran Keitel's orders.

Rudenko turned to the '*Nacht und Nebel*' directives regarding insurrection in the occupied Soviet territories: 'One must bear in mind that in the countries affected human life has absolutely no value and that a deterrent effect can be achieved only through the application of extraordinarily harsh measures.'

He turned to Keitel and asked him: 'Do you consider that necessity demanded this extremely evil order?' When Keitel attempted to qualify his answer, Rudenko continued to quote from the document: 'To atone for the life of one German soldier, 50 to 100 Communists must, as a rule, be sentenced to death. The method of execution should strengthen the measure of determent.'

Keitel claimed that his order had originally said 'five to ten' and that Hitler had added the zeroes. The implication was clear to Tribunal President Lawrence, who interjected: 'Was the only difference between you and Hitler a question of figures?'

Following Rudenko's effective and efficient cross-examination, Maxwell Fyfe once again produced the eloquent final blows. He asked Keitel to 'tell us some of the worst matters in which you acted against the inner voice of your conscience'. One of his responses related to *Nacht und Nebel* and 'the actual consequences it entailed'. Maxwell Fyfe responded with a letter from Himmler demanding that Keitel surrender 24,000 non-German civilians who were 'under arrest or held for interrogation' to the SS. Maxwell Fyfe was sceptical when Keitel declared that this was 'a misinterpretation ... police custody was meant'.

'Surely you have been at this Trial too long to think that handing people over to the SD [SS] means police custody,' he barked. 'It means a concentration camp and a gas chamber usually, does it not?'

Keitel's appearance concluded with two witnesses who were questioned by the prosecution regarding their affidavits on the Stalag Luft III massacre. Both General Adolf Westhoff and former local SS chief Max Wielen confirmed their testimonies, heaping further guilt on the defendant. Keitel's defence posed a number of procedural problems for the Tribunal. It had taken seven days and yet every single piece of documentary evidence produced had already been introduced to the court. Both prosecution and defence counsels blamed one another for the inefficiency and hoped that the judges would intervene. Privately, they believed the trial would now last until at least the end of August 1946.

CHAPTER 9

Discord Within the Defence

At ten o'clock in the morning of 11 April 1946, on the 105th day of the Nuremberg Trials, the courtroom prepared to hear the defence for SS man Ernst Kaltenbrunner. The 'big guns' – Göring, Hess, Ribbentrop and Keitel – had now been dealt with and public interest in Nuremberg once more began to wane.

In the early days of the trial there had been reasonable accord among the defendants, even if there was no shortage of mutual antipathy – often forming along the lines of Party, military and social status. But as new witnesses emerged it was possible to detect a slow shift in attitude, as some of these accused became willing to incriminate their co-defendants if they thought it might help with their plight.

In the courtroom, Göring, with his haughty, authoritative air, still carried himself as the de facto leader of the group. Two months earlier, to prevent defendants discussing their cases among themselves, the Tribunal had taken a decision to ban the prisoners from taking lunch together, so thereafter they were divided into groups of four. However, fearing that Göring was still too strong an influence, he was forced to eat in isolation.

The defence proceedings for the remaining individuals were sometimes overshadowed by shambolic examinations, repetitive evidence and verbose responses from the defendants. Everyone in the Allied camp felt the trial was dragging on longer than they had expected or thought necessary. In spite of discussions between the

Looking down on the Nuremberg courtroom.

prosecutors and the judges to make haste, however, the hearings continued to crawl along.

Ernst Kaltenbrunner

The defence of the highest-ranking member of the SS on trial, Ernst Kaltenbrunner, was despatched in barely two days, aided once more by the general non-participation of the French prosecution in these stages. A giant of a man with a thuggish demeanour, when stripped of his former power Kaltenbrunner had been effectively cowed by his incarceration. As one of the architects of the Holocaust, the indictment against Kaltenbrunner had been perhaps more damning than for any other defendant.

Like Keitel, Kaltenbrunner did not deny any of the crimes levelled against him, but simply refused to admit that they were anything to do with him. Instead, he hid behind Heinrich Himmler, head of the SS, and Heinrich Müller, chief of the Gestapo: 'I have never had authority to sign on my own initiative a so-called order for execution ... Apart from Hitler nobody in the whole Reich had such authority except Himmler and the Reich Minister of Justice.'

Press reports revealed that those present were taken aback at Kaltenbrunner's display of what were clearly barefaced lies when he was presented with a list of charges by United States prosecutor Colonel John Amen. The prosecutor began reading the damning testimonies:

> 'Testimony ... has been given here ... to the effect that you witnessed executions at Mauthausen ... the program for the extermination of Jews ... the program for forced labour ... the razing of the Warsaw Ghetto ... the execution of 50 fliers in connection with Stalag Luft III.'

The list seemed endless. Kaltenbrunner denied all of the accusations, point by point, and one by one Amen provided documentary evidence refuting his claims. Affidavits showed that he had attended Mauthausen concentration camp on a number of occasions and that on one occasion:

'Kaltenbrunner went laughing into the gas chamber. Then the people were brought from the bunker to be executed, and then all three kinds of executions: hanging, shooting in the back of the neck and gassing, were demonstrated. After the dust had disappeared we had to take away the bodies.'

Perhaps most damning of all, even Kaltenbrunner's co-defendants were disgusted by his performance.

One of the most notorious witnesses to be called before the Tribunal was Rudolf Höss (not to be confused with defendant Rudolf Hess). The commandant at the Auschwitz extermination camp might have seemed like an unlikely defence witness, yet if he was prepared to take responsibility for the murder of millions of Jews that burden could perhaps be lifted from Kaltenbrunner. He was introduced by Kaltenbrunner's counsel, Dr Kauffmann:

'Witness, your statements will have far-reaching significance. You are perhaps the only one who can throw some light upon certain hidden aspects, and who can tell which people gave the orders for the destruction of European Jewry, and can further state how this order was carried out and to what degree the execution was kept a secret.'

Höss's interrogation gave a unique insight into the workings of the death camps. As far as he was concerned, he was a technician with a job to do – a job that he took pride in carrying out as efficiently as possible:

'I visited Treblinka to find out how they carried out their exterminations. The camp commandant at Treblinka told me that he had liquidated 80,000 in the course of one half year ... He used monoxide gas ... I did not think that his methods were very efficient. So when I set up the extermination building at Auschwitz, I used Zyklon B which ... we dropped into the death chamber from a small opening. It took from 3 to 15 minutes to kill the people in the death chamber, depending upon climatic conditions. We knew when the people were dead because their screaming stopped. We usually waited about one half hour before we opened the doors and removed the bodies. After the bodies were removed our special Kommandos took off the rings and extracted the gold from the teeth of the corpses.'

Höss took the greatest pride in creating a camp that outperformed Treblinka:

'We built our gas chamber to accommodate 2,000 people at one time whereas at Treblinka their 10 gas chambers only accommodated 200 people each ... Those who were fit for work were sent into the camp. Others were sent immediately to the extermination plants. Children of tender years were invariably exterminated since by reason of their youth they were unable to work ... At Auschwitz we endeavoured to fool the victims into thinking that they were to go through a delousing process. Of course, frequently they realized our true intentions ... Very frequently women would hide their children under their clothes, but of course when we found them we would send the children in to be exterminated. We were required to carry out these exterminations in secrecy but of course the foul and nauseating stench from the continuous burning of bodies permeated the entire area and all of the people living in the surrounding communities knew that exterminations were going on at Auschwitz.'

The defence tried to argue that many of the decrees for mass executions had been illegally signed in Kaltenbrunner's name by Gestapo chief Heinrich Müller. Colonel Amen, however, had little difficulty in getting Höss to agree that Müller was simply signing them as Kaltenbrunner's representative.

Höss would later be tried and hanged in Warsaw, but his testimony at Nuremberg would provide the most detailed, and horrific, account of the workings of the Nazi death camps.

Alfred Rosenberg

The defence of Alfred Rosenberg, one of the architects of Nazi racial theory, was frustrating for everyone present. He had been the author of the seminal Nazi work, *The Myth of the Twentieth Century*, notoriously a book the Führer himself deemed too difficult to read. Göring had branded it 'philosophical belching', a description that could very easily have been applied to his own testimony. The charges against Rosenberg, however, were mostly in connection with his time as minister for the occupied Eastern Territories. He offered little in the way of defending the charges against him and took every opportunity to launch into meandering abstract thoughts. The press reported that 'those who could went to get coffee or took an early lunch'.

Hans Frank

There was also little to be said in the defence of Hans Frank. Hitler's former lawyer had provided the ultimate gift of self-incrimination by offering more than 40 volumes of his personal diaries. Furthermore, he would offer no personal defence. Confessing to some of the charges levelled against him, he was – along with Albert Speer – one of only two of the defendants to display any remorse or penitence. Asked by his counsel, Dr Seidl, if he had participated in the extermination of the Jews, he gave a surprising response:

> 'Having lived through the five months of this trial, and particularly after having heard the testimony of the witness Höss, my conscience does not allow me to throw the responsibility solely on these minor people. I myself have never installed an extermination camp for Jews, or promoted the existence of such camps; but if Adolf Hitler personally has laid that dreadful responsibility on his people, then it is mine too, for we have fought against Jewry for years; and we have indulged in the most horrible utterances – my own diary

bears witness against me. Therefore, it is no more than my duty to answer your question in this connection with "yes". A thousand years will pass and still this guilt of Germany will not have been erased.'

Frank's admission on Thursday, 18 April 1946 divided the defendants and some were now beinning to contemplate making accusations against each other. They would have time to consider their actions as the Tribunal adjourned for Easter.

Wilhelm Frick

The Minister of the Interior from 1933 to 1943, Frick had played a key role in the suppression of opposition within Germany during the early days of Hitler's rise to power. As a lawyer he had been instrumental in the creation of the Nuremberg Laws. Like Rudolf Hess, Frick chose not to take the stand himself. His defence counsel Dr Otto Pannenbecker sought to clarify the differences between 'formal authority and actual responsibility' but made no denial of the charges against him.

The most interesting aspect of Frick's defence was the witness called upon to testify on his behalf. Hans Bernd Gisevius was an unusual man. After joining the Gestapo in 1933 he quickly developed disagreements with senior figures and soon became a covert opponent of the Nazis, compiling dossiers on illegal activities from his position within the Abwehr, the German intelligence service. His role in the defence was ostensibly to show that Frick had no executive power, but he was also there as a defence witness for Schacht. His presence certainly unnerved the other defendants, who feared what he might reveal during his three-day examination.

In the event, very little of Gisevius's testimony offered any assistance to Frick. Robert Jackson conducted the cross-examination and took the opportunity to quiz him about the other defendants. It was a gift for the prosecution. As an opponent of Hitler, Schacht came off well, being described by Gisevius as a 'proponent of decency and justice'. Keitel was, he claimed, familiar with the use of slave labour and the extermination of the Jews and also 'occupied one of the most influential positions in the Third Reich ... [he] decided which documents were to be transmitted to Hitler'.

And there were some who certainly had more influence over the Führer than they might have claimed:

> 'Take the Defendant Jodl, for instance. I would like to call your attention to the strange influence which this defendant had and the position he had with regard to controlling access to Hitler ... Funk, without a doubt, had access to Hitler for a long time, and for his part Funk had of course the responsibility to see that affairs in the Ministry of Economics and in the Reichsbank were conducted in the way Hitler desired. Without a doubt Funk put his surpassingly expert knowledge at the service of Hitler.'

It was Göring, however, who received the most opprobriation from Gisevius. Göring may not have planned the Reichstag fire – that was Goebbels – but he certainly knew the details of the plan and he had also ordered the murder of one of the SA men responsible for carrying out the attack. The man had foolishly told a magistrate that he had not been paid for the job. According to Gisevius: 'The SA man, named Rall, who betrayed the plan, was murdered in a vile manner with the knowledge of the Defendant Göring, by order of Gestapo chief Diels.'

Gisevius was also able to cast light on Göring's role in the squalid affairs of Field Marshals Blomberg and Fritsch, both of whom were high-ranking figures who had opposed aggressive war. They were both removed from their positions after Göring had conspired to have damaging personal information passed to Hitler, whether real or false: Blomberg had married a former prostitute with a criminal record, it was said, and Fritsch had been falsely accused of being a homosexual.

Not for the first time at Nuremberg, an attempted defence witness had been turned into an unexpected triumph for the prosecution.

Julius Streicher

Loathed by his co-defendants, who viewed him as stupid and uncouth and detested his practice of exercising naked, Julius Streicher had been an anti-Semitic rabble-rouser, producing horribly inflammatory articles in his newspaper *Der Stürmer*. The case against Streicher was weak, however. His work might have been considered an incitement to attack Germany's Jewish population, but within the context of the Tribunal it was hard to prove that he had committed crimes, or that anyone else had committed a crime as a direct result of reading *Der Stürmer*.

Streicher might have been better off not taking the stand, but his ego, it seems, got the better of him. He immediately launched into an attack on his defence counsel, Dr Hans Marx, declaring that he 'has not conducted and was not in a position to conduct my defence in the way I wanted'. The disgruntled Marx responded that if Streicher thought him incapable then he should ask for another defence counsel, but Lawrence would have none of it and told them they should proceed with the case.

Much of Streicher's testimony was little more than anti-Semitic ranting, but as detestable as he might have been personally, the case against him still seemed thin. Six defence witnesses were offered, all of whom provided little of substance, including his young wife, and the prosecution saw no need for cross-examination.

Hjalmar Schacht

Much the most intellectual of the defendants, in his diaries psychologist Gilbert described Hjalmar Schacht, the former president of the Reichsbank, as 'a brilliant mentality'. Schacht took the witness box on 30 April – the 117th day of the trial. Following an almost glowing earlier testimony by witness Gisevius, the other defendants had turned against him. Like Streicher – albeit for reasons that could not have been any more different – the case against him was looking slim. Even though his brilliant work as a banker and economist had aided Hitler, he had never been a member of the Nazi Party himself although initially he had shared a common aim with the organization, to end the Weimar Republic. For one thing, he objected to the presence of Socialist Party elements in the government, because he saw them as an impediment to Germany's financial recovery. However, he bore the Jews no ill will. In 1937 he was removed as Reich Minister for Economics and no longer held great influence with Hitler or the Nazis. By the start of the war,

Schacht had started making contact with the German resistance and at the end of hostilities he was an inmate at Dachau.

Schacht began his defence with an eloquent assessment of Hitler:

'I have spoken of Hitler as a semi-educated man ... He did not have sufficient school education, but he read an enormous amount later, and acquired a wide knowledge. He juggled with that knowledge in a masterly manner in all debates, discussions, and speeches. No doubt he was a man of genius in certain respects. He had sudden ideas of which nobody else had thought and which were at times useful in solving great difficulties, sometimes with astounding simplicity, sometimes, however, with equally astounding brutality. He was a mass psychologist of really diabolical genius ... He was a man of unbending energy, of a will power which overcame all obstacles, and in my estimate only those two characteristics – mass psychology and his energy and will power – explain that Hitler was able to rally up to 40 percent, and later almost 50 percent, of the German people behind him.'

Throughout, the core of Schacht's defence was to establish his credentials as someone who had shared certain legitimate aims with Hitler, in particular the restoration of the German economy, while at the same time making it clear that he had no time for the Nazis, and actively abhorred and worked against some of their actions. And it was patriotism that had caused him to remain in government positions for such a long time. Much of what he claimed had already been backed up by the testimony of witness Gisevius.

On 2 May 1946, Schacht faced a cross-examination by Robert Jackson, who hoped to re-establish himself after faring so poorly against Hermann Göring. His aim was to prove beyond doubt the conspiracy case against Schacht. He began well, showing that although the defendant had not been a member of the Nazi Party he had nonetheless been given the honour of the Party's golden swastika and that he did wear it on 'official occasions'. (It was 'very convenient on railroad journeys, when ordering a car'.) Also, Schacht could not deny that he contributed 1,000 Reichsmarks a year to the Party from 1937 to 1942.

Jackson sought to show that a large part of the New Plan, which Schacht had introduced in 1934 as a means of achieving German economic self-sufficiency, had been in aid of Germany's rearmament programme. Although Schacht denied that there was a link, Jackson cited a 1938 speech where he had told his audience: 'These figures show how much the New Plan contributed to the execution of the armament program as well as to the securing of our food.'

On matters of economics, Jackson could not hope to compete with Schacht's experience and expertise and so largely gave up trying. He was, however, able to use Schacht to provide ammunition against other defendants – Göring in particular, with whom Schacht admitted to being at odds on many issues. Jackson referred to a pre-trial interrogation with British intelligence officer Major Edmund Tilley, in which Schacht described Göring's eccentric behaviour:

'In his personal appearance he was so theatrical that one could only compare him with Nero. A lady who had tea with his second wife reported that he appeared at this tea in a sort of Roman toga and sandals studded with jewels, his fingers bedecked with innumerable jewelled rings and generally covered with ornaments, his face painted and his lips rouged.

'Whereas I have called Hitler an amoral type of person, I can regard Göring only as immoral and criminal. Endowed by nature with a certain geniality which he managed to exploit for his own popularity, he was the most egocentric being imaginable. The assumption of political power was for him only a means to personal enrichment and personal good living. The success of others filled him with envy. His greed knew no bounds ... He knew no comradeship. Only as long as someone was useful to him did he profess friendship.'

Schacht then brought into question Göring's abilities, claiming that his 'knowledge in all fields in which a government member should be competent was nil, especially in the economic field. Of all the economic matters which Hitler entrusted to him in the autumn of 1936 he had not the faintest notion.'

At the end of the defence, both Jackson and Schacht considered themselves happy with the outcome. Jackson may not have inflicted the heavy defeat on the defendant he might have liked, but his reputation had been somewhat rehabilitated. On the other hand, Schacht was so convinced of the outcome that he prepared himself for acquittal.

Walther Funk

Just as he had followed Hjalmar Schacht to the pinnacle of Germany's financial system, Walther Funk followed Schacht into the witness box. Unlike his predecessor, Funk presided over the Reichsbank for the entirety of the war and found himself indicted on all four charges. Funk's defence testimony was weak and peppered with periods of weeping. When prosecutor Dodd took over on 6 May, he began by ascertaining whether Funk had admitted any wrongdoing in his earlier testimony:

'You admit none of the charges made against you in the Indictment in any degree, with possibly one exception ... Would you tell us now whether or not you intended to admit your own guilt or the part that you played in the persecution of the Jews?'

Funk replied that he was merely acting under orders.

'I said this morning that I had a deep sense of guilt and a deep sense of shame about the things which were done to the Jews in Germany. I did not feel guilty in respect to the Indictment against me here ... because I signed the directives for carrying out laws which had been issued by superior officers ... I am admitting a guilt against myself, a moral guilt, but not a guilt because I signed the directives for carrying out the laws.'

With regard to the looting of Jewish property, Dodd turned to an affidavit from Emil Puhl, vice president of the Reichsbank:

'Funk told me that he had arranged with Reichsführer Himmler to have the Reichsbank receive in safe custody gold and jewels for the SS ... I asked Funk what the source was of the gold, jewels, banknotes, and other articles to be delivered by the SS. Funk replied that it was confiscated property from the Eastern Occupied Territories, and that I should ask no further questions ... The material deposited by the SS included jewelry, watches, eyeglass frames, dental gold, and other gold articles in great abundance, taken by the SS from Jews, concentration camp victims, and other persons. This was brought to our knowledge by SS personnel who attempted to convert this material into cash and who were helped in this by the Reichsbank personnel with Funk's approval and knowledge.'

'Did you ever,' Dodd asked Funk, 'hear of anybody depositing his gold dentures in a bank for safekeeping?'

Karl Dönitz

Grand Admiral of the German Navy since 1943, Karl Dönitz's defence counsel was naval judge Flottenrichter Otto Kranzbühler, a figure who had already impressed the assembled legal brains on display at Nuremberg. There had been a degree of sympathy for both naval leaders on trial – Dönitz and Erich Raeder – whose alleged wrongdoings were not deemed to be on the same scale as the other wings of the military or the SS and the Gestapo. Dönitz saw himself as a professional sailor who had no view on whether he was engaged in aggressive war:

'I received military orders as a soldier, and my purpose naturally was to carry out these military tasks. Whether the leadership of the State was thereby politically waging an aggressive war or not, or whether they were protective measures, was not for me to decide; it was none of my business.'

He was questioned in particular about the use of U-boats on merchant shipping. 'The Prosecution has repeatedly termed the U-boat arm an aggressive weapon,' remarked Kranzbühler. 'What do you say to this?'

Dönitz agreed that it was.

'Do you mean to say by that that it is a weapon for an aggressive war?' Kranzbühler continued.

'Aggressive or defensive war is a political decision,' Dönitz countered. 'It has nothing to do with military considerations. I can certainly use a U-boat in a defensive war because, in defensive war also, the enemy's ships must be attacked. Of course, I can use a U-boat in exactly the same way in a politically aggressive war. If one should conclude that the navies which have U-boats are planning an aggressive war, then all nations – for all the navies of these nations had U-boats, in fact many had more than Germany, twice and three times as many – planned aggressive war.'

Furthermore, if Dönitz were to be found guilty of carrying out unrestricted submarine warfare in violation of international agreements then the same charge would surely have to be levelled at the United States.

When Sir David Maxwell Fyfe cross-examined Dönitz, he began by establishing his National Socialist credentials – his 'fanatical adherence to Hitler and to the Party' – and how he'd sought 'to indoctrinate the Navy with Nazi ideology'. He quoted Dönitz:

> 'From the very start the whole of the officers' corps must be so indoctrinated that it feels itself co-responsible for the National Socialist State in its entirety. The officer is the exponent of the State. The idle chatter that the officer is non-political is sheer nonsense.'

Maxwell Fyfe then quoted from a speech that Dönitz gave on Heroes' Day, in 1944:

> 'What would have become of our country today if the Führer had not united us under National Socialism? Split parties, beset

with the spreading poison of Jewry, and vulnerable to it because
we lacked the defense of our present uncompromising ideology,
we would long since have succumbed under the burden of this
war and delivered ourselves up to the enemy who would have
mercilessly destroyed us.'

Erich Raeder

The charges of conspiracy and waging an aggressive war would perhaps
be easier for the prosecution to execute in the case of Grand Admiral
Raeder. For a start, his military career had been longer than that of
Dönitz, who had led the German Navy between 1928 and 1943. The
prosecution claimed that he had attended two conferences that made
Hitler's aggressive war intentions plain: on 5 November 1937 Hitler
talked of the taking of Austria and Czechoslovakia and had declared that
rearmament was still moving too slowly; and on 23 May 1939 Hitler had
said that Poland would have to be attacked at a suitable opportunity.

Maxwell Fyfe provided documents demonstrating that the rebuilding
of the German Navy during the 1930s had violated the terms imposed
on Germany by the Treaty of Versailles. U-boats might have been built
in Germany within those limitations but

> 'as early as 1922, three German shipbuilding yards established
> a German U-boat designing office in Holland under a Dutch
> cover name with about 30 engineers and designers ... In 1925
> a Dutch shipbuilding yard built two 500-ton U-boats for Turkey
> according to the plans of this bureau, which enjoyed the financial
> and personal support of the Naval Command.'

One of these boats, 'the Turkish submarine *Guer* became the prototype
for the U-25 and U-26'.

Germany claimed that it had 55 U-boats ready for action in 1938:
'In reality 118 were completed and under construction.' Maxwell Fyfe
and Raeder discussed these numbers endlessly, the defendant becoming
increasingly evasive and agitated. Continuing with violations of the
Versailles Treaty, Maxwell Fyfe pointed out that the Treaty limited the

number of naval personnel to 15,000 men, whereas by 1935 34,000 had been trained.

Baldur von Schirach

Hitler Youth leader (and later governor of Vienna) Baldur von Schirach began his testimony on 23 May 1946 – the 137th day of the trial. His testimony began to grate with Tribunal President Lawrence almost from the beginning. He talked at length about his upbringing, his university education and the books he had read – before Lawrence interjected: 'We do not want to know the full story of the defendant's education ... we are not interested!'

Schirach's testimony was notable because it was perhaps the most vicious denouncement of Hitler to be heard at the trial. He spoke of his worsening relationship with Hitler, that had begun with the Führer's complaints about an exhibition of decadent art he had presented in Vienna. After presenting himself as a once fervent Nazi who had lost faith when he began to realize the plight of the Jews, he was asked about his reaction to the testimony of Höss, the commandant of Auschwitz:

'It is the greatest, the most devilish mass murder known to history ... Höss was merely the executioner. The murder was ordered by Adolf Hitler ... He and Himmler jointly committed that crime which, for all time, will be a stain in the annals of our history. It is a crime which fills every German with shame.'

He continued, defending his beloved Hitler Youth:

'The youth of Germany is guiltless. Our youth was anti-Semitically inclined, but it did not call for the extermination of Jewry. It neither realized nor imagined that Hitler had carried out this extermination by the daily murder of thousands of innocent people. The youth of Germany who, today, stand perplexed among the ruins of their native land, knew nothing of these crimes, nor did they desire them. They are innocent of all that Hitler has done to the Jewish and to the German people.'

He concluded this question with a statement of his own personal guilt:

'I have educated this generation in faith and loyalty to Hitler ... I believed that I was serving a leader who would make our people and the youth of our country great and happy and free ... Before God, before the German nation, and before my German people I alone bear the guilt of having trained our young people for a man whom I for many long years had considered unimpeachable, both as a leader and as the head of the State, of creating for him a generation who saw him as I did.

'The guilt is mine in that I educated the youth of Germany for a man who murdered by the millions ... This is my own – my own personal guilt. I was responsible for the youth of the country. I was placed in authority over the young people, and the guilt is mine alone. The younger generation is guiltless. It grew up in an anti-Semitic state, ruled by anti-Semitic laws ... I remained true to my oath as an officer, a youth leader, and an official ... I was a convinced National Socialist from my earliest days – as such, I was also an anti-Semite. Hitler's racial policy was a crime which led to disaster for five million Jews and for all the Germans. The younger generation bears no guilt. But he who, after Auschwitz, still clings to racial politics has rendered himself guilty.}

Schirach would declare himself satisfied with his defence. He thought he might now escape the fate surely destined for the worst Nazi criminals and instead face a life of imprisonment.

Fritz Sauckel

Although Ernst Friedrich 'Fritz' Sauckel had enjoyed a range of ministerial roles, the charges he faced at Nuremberg were mainly connected with his work as the Plenipotentiary for Labour Mobilization, namely the acquisition of workers from occupied territories. And there were few illusions as to what that meant in practice:

'The foreign workers in the Reich and the population in the occupied territories who are being employed for the German war effort must be given the feeling that it is to their own interests to work loyally for Germany and that therein alone will they see and actually find their one real guarantee of life.'

Sauckel's defence had been evasive and was easily undermined by some effective cross-examination from French prosecutor Jacques Herzog. Sauckel denied he ever used the army for the recruitment of labour, but Herzog showed him a letter indicating otherwise.

'Did you ever consider that a worker could be taken to his work handcuffed?' Herzog enquired.

'No!' came the reply. 'I never thought of such a thing ... I hear now for the first time that I am supposed to have sent, or had workers sent to their places of work handcuffed. I do not remember that. In any case, I never decreed anything like that; that much I can say.'

A few moments later, he added: '... only if there were flagrant resistance to an executive authority.'

Sauckel denied knowledge of atrocities that might have taken place at Buchenwald. He had previously testified that he visited once 'in the company of an Italian Commons'. Herzog then pulled out a photograph showing Sauckel at Buchenwald ... standing next to no less than Heinrich Himmler, the head of the SS. He then added incredulously: 'And you contend that you ... visited the Buchenwald Concentration Camp in the company of the Reichsführer SS, and – I call your attention to this – in the company of the commander of the camp, without knowledge of what was happening inside the camp?'

Soviet prosecutor Alexandrov then engaged Sauckel in an ill-tempered battle of numbers, a 'shouting match', the *Times* newspaper claimed. There were at least seven million slave labourers brought to Germany but at the end of the war there were only five million. Alexandrov suggested that 'a large number perished as a result of hard slave labour'. Sauckel nevertheless claimed, somewhat surprisingly, that they had simply 'returned to their home countries'.

Sauckel's defence team also called a number of witnesses, the main purpose of which was to play down the significance of his role and emphasize that it was Speer who was really running the show. As with previous witnesses, this largely backfired. Dr Wilhelm Jaeger, a doctor at one of the Krupp factories, attested to the appalling conditions in which foreign labourers were kept. They had survived on condemned meat (*Freibankfleisch*) and were 'housed in dog kennels, latrines, and old baking ovens'. By the end of Sauckel's defence his conviction seemed to be a certainty.

Alfred Jodl

Keitel's deputy, Alfred Jodl, would throughout the Tribunal maintain his total innocence of the charges brought against him. Indeed, he was convinced that he would be acquitted. When asked his opinion on the Jewish question, he showed no signs of anti-Semitism: 'I am of the opinion that no party, no state, no people, and no race – not even cannibals – are good or bad in themselves, but only the single individual.'

Jodl ran into difficulties when describing his reservations about the *Kommandobefehl* (Commando Order) – the instruction that Allied special forces captured during raids or acts of sabotage, 'who do not act like soldiers but like bandits', operated outside the terms of the Geneva Convention and could therefore be executed. Although he agreed with the principle he was opposed to Goebbels' suggestion that they should be lynched. Yet he had accepted Hitler's draft and distributed the document, claiming that he had no choice: 'For the ethical code of my action, I must say that it was obedience.'

Under cross-examination from British prosecutor Roberts, the hot-tempered Jodl gave a combative performance, frequently raising his voice – so much so that Lawrence stepped in and insisted that he stop shouting.

Roberts offered an array of incriminating documents, concluding: 'You will notice that of all the documents I have put forward, except for that one American report, they were all German documents ... In the face of those documents, do you still say that you are an honourable soldier and a truthful man?'

'Not only do I still affirm that,' came Jodl's retort, 'but I also think that the submission of these documents has actually and quite specifically proved it.'

Arthur Seyss-Inquart

Charged with all four counts, Seyss-Inquart began his defence on 10 June 1946, the 151st day of the trial. A politician in the Austrian government, he was accused of effectively facilitating the *Anschluss*, the annexation of his country. Later, as Reich commissioner of the Netherlands, he was charged with deporting Jews to Auschwitz, slave labour to Germany and exploiting the country's economic resources for the benefit of Germany.

It was this role that French prosecutor Delphin Debenest began to probe, asking first about the dismantling of the Dutch administration.

'I did not remove any mayors from office until they became unbearable for me because of their actively hostile attitude,' Seyss-Inquart replied.

Debenest noted that action had been taken against Dutch newspapers:

'The press was under fairly strict control by the Propaganda Ministry. The editors were employed after being judged suitable by the Netherlands Propaganda Ministry. I believe that it is a matter of course for an occupying power that for such an important instrument one takes only people who have a certain positive attitude ... I know that once in The Hague the editor's office of a newspaper was blown up.'

Seyss-Inquart found it difficult to counter claims that he had closed down universities or interfered with their operation. Debenest drew from a report: 'Attempts were made to make the University of Leyden a National Socialist university by appointing National Socialist professors. However, these attempts failed as a result of the firm attitude taken by the professors and by the students.' It continued to say how certain professors were investigated and sent to Sint-Michielsgestel concentration camp.

Dr Arthur Seyss-Inquart, the last Chancellor of Austria before the Anschluss, *delivers a speech in 1942.*

Seyss-Inquart was dismissive: 'That is this concentration camp where the inmates played golf.'

A further document was introduced showing that he had approved the shooting of 230 Dutchmen in reprisals for an assassination attempt on one of his staff. Seyss-Inquart gave a qualified response:

'I myself never ordered a single shooting. But I would like to repeat: If, for instance, I called the attention of the Police to the fact that in any certain locality of the Netherlands an illegal resistance movement was causing much trouble, and gave the Police instructions to investigate the case, it was perfectly obvious to me that the leaders of the resistance movement could be arrested by the Police who, on the basis of the Fuehrer decree, would shoot them ... but I also maintain my own declaration to the effect that I never even would have had the power to give an order like that.'

Franz von Papen

An aristocrat 'born on soil which has been in the possession of my family for 900 years', Franz von Papen followed a military career that saw him end the First World War with the rank of lieutenant colonel. He then entered German politics. Briefly appointed Chancellor by President Hindenburg in June 1932, he had been central to Hitler coming to power in 1933, in spite of being opposed to Nazi methods.

Sir David Maxwell Fyfe handled the cross-examination, beginning with the statement he had made earlier to the prosecution that Hitler was 'the greatest crook' he had ever seen in his life.

'That is the opinion which I arrived at after I learned here of all the crimes,' Papen agreed.

'"Only after I had known the facts after which he started to go to war?" Do you remember saying that?' Maxwell Fyfe asked.

Papen agreed.

'Was not that rather a long time for you to discover that somewhat obvious truth after your close co-operation with Hitler?' The prosecutor went on to show that Hitler's intentions should have been quite clear from the very beginning.

He pressed Papen over the 'Röhm Purge':

'If you, as an ex-Chancellor of the Reich and – as you said yourself – one of the leading Catholic laymen of Germany, an ex-officer of the Imperial Army, had said at that time, "I am not going to be associated with murder, cold-blooded murder as an instrument of policy", you might at some risk to yourself have brought down the whole of this rotten regime, might you not?'

'That is possible,' Papen replied, 'but had I said it publicly, then quite probably I would have disappeared somewhere just as my associates did.' Maxwell Fyfe had surely proved his point.

Maxwell Fyfe further questioned Papen's knowledge of murders that took place in the early days of Nazi rule, concluding his cross-examination with a devastating assessment:

'The only reason that could have kept you in the service of the Nazi government when you knew of all these crimes was that you sympathized and wanted to carry on with the Nazis' work … You had seen your own friends, your own servants, murdered around you. You had the detailed knowledge of it, and the only reason that could have led you on and made you take one job after another from the Nazis was that you sympathized with their work. That is what I am putting against you, Herr von Papen.'

Albert Speer

'Fanatical on the subject of architecture', Adolf Hitler was a 'close personal contact' of Albert Speer. Although initially engaged as Hitler's personal architect, Speer faced indictments at Nuremberg for his role as Reichminister for Armaments and Munitions. And the core of those charges related to his use of forced labour, procured by Sauckel; this included violating the Hague Convention in the use of prisoners of war.

Youthful, polite and neatly dressed in a smart civilian suit, Speer cut a figure that contrasted starkly with the other defendants. His defence counsel, Dr Flachsner, first brought up the subject of his responsibility for recruiting foreign workers 'and for taking manpower from concentration camps'.

But Speer accepted no blame whatsoever. 'The fact that the SS put itself and its concentration camp internees outside the control of the State is not a matter with which I or my Ministry was concerned,' he replied.

Speer accepted that Sauckel had provided labour according to his requirements but although he might have realized that it was forced labour, how the workers were procured or treated was none of his business. Indeed, most of his defence counsel's cross-examination seemed to be focused on how impressive the young Speer's achievements had been.

Speer then discussed his efforts to end the war. With the Allied bombing of the Ruhr in May 1944: '90 percent of the fuel was lost to us from that time on. The success of these attacks meant the loss of the war as far as production was concerned; for our new tanks and jet planes were of no use without fuel.'

He then wrote to Hitler: 'I told him of this in great detail, both orally and in writing. Between June and December 1944 I sent him 12 memoranda, all with catastrophic news.'

His final assessment of Hitler was damning: 'The sacrifices which were made on both sides after January 1945 were senseless. The dead of this period will be the accusers of the man responsible for the continuation of that fight, Adolf Hitler.'

When questioned about his ultimate loyalty to Hitler, he declared that there was, 'one loyalty which everyone must always keep; and that is loyalty towards one's own people. That duty comes before everything.'

Speer went on to relate a sensational story of his plot to assassinate Hitler, by feeding poison gas into the Führerbunker through an air conditioning ventilator shaft in the Reich Chancellery garden – a story verified by the man who supplied him with the gas. But on the day of the planned assassination: 'I discovered that on Hitler's personal order this ventilator had recently been surrounded by a chimney four meters high ... Due to this it was no longer possible to carry out my plan.'

Göring was incensed. In his view, Speer deserved to be executed as a traitor.

Konstantin von Neurath

The oldest of the accused, Neurath began his defence on 22 June 1946. By the time the Nazis came to power, Neurath had already enjoyed a notable diplomatic career and he would go on to serve as Hitler's Foreign Minister from 1932 to 1938. Affidavits were provided by the defence to show that Neurath was not anti-Semitic. Baroness Hitter noted:

'The same tolerant attitude which he had towards Christian denominations he also had towards the Jewish question. Therefore, he rejected Hitler's racial policy as a matter of principle. In practice he also succeeded in preventing any elimination of Jews under his jurisdiction until the year 1937.'

Central to Neurath's defence was that he only held his position until 1938, when he was removed following his opposition to Hitler's plans for waging aggressive war. It was his successor, Ribbentrop, who was more culpable for the atrocities that took place. He himself regarded the war, he said, 'as the greatest piece of stupidity'.

Neurath, it was claimed, harboured doubts over Hitler's personality and furthermore had never been a Nazi Party member: 'I despised the methods of the Party during its struggle for power in the State.'

Answering charges that he remained a part of Hitler's government knowing that the Party had been behind the murder of Ernst Röhm, he declared:

'I never belonged to a party; I never swore allegiance to party programs, and I never swore any allegiance to party leaders either. I served under the Imperial Government ... I have pursued only the interests of my Fatherland in co-operation with the other powers ... There was no reason for me not to attempt to do the same under Hitler and the National Socialist Party. One could put opposition opinions into effect with any prospect of success only from the inside as a member of the Government.'

Cross-examiner Maxwell Fyfe was unconvinced: 'Why did you go on in a government that was using murder as an instrument of political action?'

Neurath's response seemed somewhat blasé: 'In the case of such revolutions such mishaps cannot be avoided, most unfortunately.'

Following the annexation of Czechoslovakia, Neurath had been appointed Reichsprotektor. Evidence was presented that Neurath had suggested that:

> 'The most radical and theoretically complete solution to the problem would be to evacuate all Czechs completely from this country and replace them by Germans ... keeping those Czechs who are suitable for Germanization by individual selective breeding, while on the other hand expelling those who are not useful from a racial standpoint or are enemies of the Reich.'

His flustered response was that the document was written by Frank and that his name had been added.

Hans Fritzsche

Wednesday, 26 June 1946 saw the final defendant enter the witness box. There had been talk at Nuremberg of dropping the Fritzsche case altogether. He was just a lowly Nazi journalist who made propaganda radio broadcasts and kept the press in line. Fritzsche had not met Hitler and neither did he know any of the other defendants, although he was said to have been popular among them in prison and had helped them with their presentations. There was a common view that Fritzsche was there simply as a proxy for the deceased Dr Goebbels – the Nazi master of propaganda. Moreover, except for the same kind of incitement claims that had been made against Streicher, the prosecution case against him was weak. His defence counsel, Dr Fritz, set the scene: Fritzsche held no official Party post and no official political post; and he had never been a member of 'the SA or the SS or any one of the other organizations which are accused here'. An additional problem facing the prosecution was that Fritzsche's radio broadcasts were not prepared pieces but largely improvised, and recordings were never made, so no documentary evidence existed.

From the very beginning, the prosecution cross-examination was clutching at straws. General Rudenko first tried to elicit an admission that the Nazi use of propaganda had contributed to the Holocaust.

'I admit,' replied Fritzsche, 'that German propaganda spread the racial theory but I deny most emphatically that German propaganda had made preparations for, or had called for, the mass murder of Jews.'

He finally gave a damning verdict on Hitler and National Socialism, declaring 'three fundamental mistakes … the trust in Adolf Hitler's humaneness, which was destroyed by the order to murder five million people; the second, the trust in the ethical purity of the system, which was destroyed by the orders to apply torture; and the third, the absolute trust in Adolf Hitler's peaceful intentions, shaken by what has been brought up in this courtroom.'

Martin Bormann

Something of a farcical postscript, the defence of Martin Bormann, being tried *in absentia*, took barely half a day, slotted in as it was on 29 June 1946, directly after the conclusion of Fritzsche's defence. Dr Friedrich Bergold, Bormann's elected counsel, announced to the Tribunal that nearly all of the witnesses he had requested – who would have been there to testify that Bormann was dead – could not be found. One of them, Fraulein Christians, had been released from captivity to appear: 'She was at Camp Oberursel. She received leave and while on leave disappeared – obviously she has fled!'

CHAPTER 10

Closing Statements

The trial of the major war criminals at the International Military Tribunal at Nuremberg had taken a good deal longer than anybody had predicted at the beginning. On Thursday, 4 July 1946, the final statements for the defence began. Mindful of the urgent need to move on to the stage of the Tribunal that covered the illegal organizations that operated within Nazi Germany, the defence counsels were given explicit instructions to keep their presentations brief. Each one was allowed to take no more than half a day, the statements had to be submitted beforehand and their contents were to be cut back if the judges saw necessary. In the main, although these were summary speeches by each of the defendants' counsels, a good deal of the content was what Professor Hermann Jahrreiss, Jodl's assistant counsel, referred to as 'juridicial questions'.

Precise and scholarly, Professor Jahrreiss had been chosen to make a statement on general legal points and commenced with a detailed assessment of how international agreements cited by the prosecution – the League of Nations Covenant, the Kellogg–Briand Pact, the Hague and Geneva Conventions – did not necessarily provide a legal basis for the personal indictments set out in the Charter of London. After several hours, Jahrreiss reached his conclusion:

'Sentences against individuals for breach of the peace between states would be something completely new under the aspect of law, something revolutionarily new ... Sentences against individuals for breach of the peace between states presuppose other laws than those in force when the actions laid before this Tribunal took place. The legal question of guilt – and I am here only concerned with that – is thus posed in its full complexity for not one of the defendants could have held even one of the two views of the legal world constitution, on which the chief prosecutors base their arguments.'

He argued that the differing legal systems between the five countries created unique problems ('the concept of conspiracy as used by the Prosecution is entirely unknown to German law'); that as victors, 'the penal law contained in the [London] Charter is ex post facto penal law'. This meant that the laws or consequences of the violations had been either created or changed after the event to suit the Allies – he cited the waging of aggressive war as something condemned by Kellogg–Briand, but which was not a violation. In short, without a law having previously existed, there could be neither crime nor punishment, the principle of 'nullum crimen sine lege' (no crime without law).

He then moved on to Adolf Hitler and the matter of how responsibility can be attributed to an individual under his rule:

'The Prosecution is based upon the conception of a conspiracy to conquer the world on the part of a few dozen criminals ... the so-called Führer Principle ... [which has] been the organizational guiding principle in the development of the Reich constitution after 1933 ... in a state in which the entire power to make final decisions is concentrated in the hands of a single individual, the orders of this one man are absolutely binding on the members of the hierarchy. This individual is their sovereign.'

Although the closing statements for the individual defendants took up most of the following three weeks, they yielded very little of interest – even to their clients – and added almost nothing to their cases. Observers and the press noted that this period was much the dullest of the entire Nuremberg spectacle. *The New Yorker* magazine later captured the mood: 'The courtroom is a citadel of boredom. Every person attending it is in the grip of extreme tedium.'

The return of Robert H. Jackson

On Friday, 26 July 1946, the first of the four closing cases for the prosecution was heard. Just as the proceedings had begun the previous November, Justice Robert H. Jackson took the entirety of the morning session to make his closing statement. Rightly celebrated for his masterful presentation at the beginning of the trial, Jackson's lustre had faded dramatically with his dismal cross-examination of Hermann Göring, who had bested him on almost every point. Jackson therefore saw this as an opportunity to rehabilitate his reputation. He wouldn't disappoint.

'An advocate can be confronted with few more formidable tasks than to select his closing arguments where there is great disparity between his appropriate time and his available material. In eight months – a short time as state trials go – we have introduced evidence which embraces as vast and varied a panorama of events as has ever been compressed within the framework of a litigation. It is impossible in summation to do more than outline with bold strokes the vitals of this Trial's mad and melancholy record, which will live as the historical text of the 20th century's shame and depravity.

'It is common to think of our own time as standing at the apex of civilization, from which the deficiencies of preceding ages may patronizingly be viewed in the light of what is assumed to be "progress". The reality is that in the long perspective of history the present century will not hold an admirable position, unless its second half is to redeem its first ... Two World Wars have left a legacy of dead which number more than all the armies engaged in any way that made ancient or medieval history. No half-century ever witnessed slaughter on such a scale, such cruelties and inhumanities, such wholesale deportations of peoples into slavery, such annihilations of minorities ... If we cannot eliminate the causes and prevent the repetition of these barbaric events, it is not an irresponsible prophecy to say that this 20th century may yet succeed in bringing the doom of civilization.'

He dismissed the defence claims regarding the legitimacy of the Tribunal. Like all criminals, he remarked:

'Their dislike for the law which condemns them is not original ... of one thing we may be sure. The future will never have to ask, with misgiving, what could the Nazis have said in their favour. History will know that whatever could be said, they were allowed to say. They have been given the kind of a Trial which they, in the days of their pomp and power, never gave to any man ... But fairness is not weakness. The extraordinary fairness of these hearings is an attribute of our strength.'

Jackson outlined the conspiracy charges and described how the Nazis had seized power, changing Germany's laws to consolidate that power and creating 'instrumentalities' like the SD (SS) and the Gestapo to subjugate opposition. He went on to discuss how they had prepared and waged wars of aggression, rearming in defiance of the Treaty of Versailles and launching unprovoked attacks; how they had enslaved and plundered the populations of occupied countries; and how they had persecuted and murdered Jews and Christians.

He was brutal in his assessment of the defendants:

'Nobody knew anything about what was going on. Time after time we have heard the chorus from the dock: "I only heard about these things here for the first time." These men saw no evil, spoke none, and none was uttered in their presence. This claim might sound very plausible if made by one defendant. But when we put all their stories together, the impression which emerges ... is ludicrous.

'The large and varied role of Goering was half militarist and half gangster. He stuck his pudgy finger in every pie. He used his SA musclemen to help bring the gang into power. In order to entrench that power he contrived to have the Reichstag burned, established the Gestapo, and created the concentration camps ... He was, next to Hitler, the man who tied the activities of all the defendants together in a common effort ... The zealot Hess ... the engineer ... supervising every aspect of Party activities ... the duplicitous Ribbentrop, the salesman of deception, who was detailed to pour wine on the troubled waters of suspicion by preaching the gospel of limited and peaceful intentions. Keitel, the weak and willing tool [who] delivered the Armed Forces ... over to the Party and directed them in executing its felonous designs. Kaltenbrunner, the grand inquisitor, took up the bloody mantle of Heydrich to stifle opposition and terrorize compliance ... Rosenberg, the intellectual high priest of the "master race", provided the doctrine of hatred which gave the impetus for the annihilation of Jewry ... The fanatical Frank, who solidified Nazi control by establishing the new order of authority without law, so that the will of the Party was the only test of legality, proceeded to export his lawlessness to Poland, which he governed with the lash of Caesar and whose population he reduced to sorrowing remnants. Frick, the ruthless organizer, helped the Party to seize power, supervised the police agencies to insure that it stayed in power, and chained the economy of Bohemia and Moravia to the German war machine. Streicher, the venomous Bulgarian, manufactured and distributed obscene racial libels which incited the populace to accept and assist the progressively savage operations of "race purification".

'As Minister of Economics Funk accelerated the pace of rearmament, and as Reichsbank president banked for the SS the gold teeth fillings of concentration camp victims – probably the most ghoulish collateral in banking history. It was Schacht, the facade of starched respectability, who in the early days provided the window dressing, the bait for the hesitant, and whose wizardry later made it possible for Hitler to finance the colossal rearmament program, and to do it secretly. Dönitz, Hitler's legatee of defeat, promoted the success of the Nazi aggressions by instructing his pack of submarine killers to conduct warfare at sea with the illegal ferocity of the jungle. Raeder, the political admiral, stealthily built up the German Navy in defiance of the Versailles Treaty, and then put it to use in a series of aggressions which he had taken a leading part in planning. Von Schirach, poisoner of a generation, initiated the German youth in Nazi doctrine, trained them in legions for service in the SS and Wehrmacht, and delivered them up to the Party as fanatic, unquestioning executors of its will.

'Sauckel, the greatest and cruellest slaver since the Pharaohs of Egypt, produced desperately needed manpower by driving foreign peoples into the land of bondage on a scale unknown even in the ancient days of tyranny in the kingdom of the Nile. Jodl, betrayer of the traditions of his profession, led the Wehrmacht in violating its own code of military honour in order to carry out the barbarous aims of Nazi policy. Von Papen, pious agent of an infidel regime, held the stirrup while Hitler vaulted into the saddle, lubricated the Austrian annexation, and devoted his diplomatic cunning to the service of Nazi objectives abroad. Seyss-Inquart, spearhead of the Austrian fifth column, took over the government of his own country only to make a present of it to Hitler ... Von Neurath, the old-school diplomat, who cast the pearls of his experience before Nazis and guided Nazi diplomacy in the early years ... Speer, as Minister of Armaments and Production, joined in planning and executing the program to dragoon prisoners of war and foreign workers into German war industries ... Fritzsche, radio propaganda chief, by manipulation of the truth goaded German public opinion into frenzied support of the regime ... And Bormann, who has not accepted our invitation to this reunion, sat at the throttle of the vast and powerful engine of the Party.'

On personal responsibility, and the *Führerprinzip* defence, Jackson spoke with absolute certainty:

'I admit that Hitler was the chief villain. But for the defendants to put all blame on him is neither manly nor true ... He must rely on others to be his eyes and ears ... other legs must run his errands ... other hands must execute his plans. On whom did Hitler rely for such things more than upon these men in the dock?

'Who led him to believe he had an invincible air armada if not Goering? Who kept disagreeable facts from him? ... Who led Hitler, utterly untraveled himself, to believe in the indecision and timidity of democratic peoples if not Ribbentrop, Von Neurath, and Von Papen? Who fed his illusion of German invincibility if not Keitel, Jodl, Raeder, and Doenitz? Who kept his hatred of the Jews inflamed more than Streicher and Rosenberg? ... They were the Praetorian Guard, and while they were under Caesar's orders, Caesar was always in their hands.

'If these dead men could take the witness stand and answer what has been said against them, we might have a less distorted picture of the parts played by these defendants. Imagine the stir that would occur in the dock if it should behold Adolf Hitler advancing to the witness box, or Himmler ... or Goebbels ... or Bormann ... The ghoulish defence that the world is entitled to retribution only from the cadavers is an argument worthy of the crimes at which it is directed.'

Robert Jackson's masterful performance ended with a wonderfully theatrical flourish as he made reference to Shakespeare's *Richard III*:

'These defendants now ask this Tribunal to say that they are not guilty of planning, executing, or conspiring to commit this long list of crimes and wrongs. They stand before the record of this Trial as bloodstained Gloucester stood by the body of his slain king. He begged of the widow, as they beg of you: "Say I slew them not." And the Queen replied, "Then say they were not slain. But dead they are ... " If you were to say of these men that they are not guilty, it would be as true to say that there has been no war, there are no slain, there has been no crime.'

Sir Hartley Shawcross

His government role as Attorney General meant that British chief prosecutor Sir Hartley Shawcross had not attended the whole of the trial. He returned, however, to give his closing address. It may have lacked the eloquence of the preceding speech, but it was at least its equal in impact. And it took up the rest of the afternoon and the whole of the following day.

Shawcross focused on dismantling the legal arguments of the defence and upholding the validity of the Charter's indictment of crimes against peace. Although the Tribunal was there to ascertain 'that each of these defendants is legally guilty', Shawcross maintained that there were broader issues at stake and produced a startling account of Nazi crimes:

'That these defendants participated in and are morally guilty of crimes so frightful that the imagination staggers and reels back at their very contemplation is not in doubt ... total and totalitarian war, waged in defiance of solemn undertakings and in breach of treaties ... great cities, from Coventry to Stalingrad, reduced to rubble, the countryside laid waste, and now the inevitable aftermath of war so fought – hunger and disease stalking through the world; millions of people homeless, maimed, bereaved ...'

'Nor was that the only or the greatest crime,' Shawcross continued. He went on to say that when a murder takes place we ensure that

'the criminal is punished and the rule of law is vindicated. Shall we do less when not one but on the lowest computation twelve million men, women and children are done to death? Not in battle, not in passion, but in the cold, calculated, deliberate attempt to destroy nations and races, to disintegrate the traditions, the institutions and the very existence of free and ancient states. Twelve million murders. Two-thirds of the

British chief prosecutor Sir Hartley Shawcross addresses the court.

Jews in Europe exterminated, more than six million of them on the killers' own figures. Murder conducted like some mass production industry in the gas chambers and the ovens of Auschwitz, Dachau, Treblinka, Buchenwald, Mauthausen, Majdanek, and Oranienburg.'

Like Jackson, Shawcross also made a brief comment on each of the defendants.

Göring – 'Behind his spurious air of bonhomie, he was as great an architect as any in this satanic system. Who, apart from Hitler, had more knowledge of what went on, or greater influence to affect its course?'

Hess – 'Not content with creating the monster [the Nazi Party], he aided it in every aspect of its monstrous work.'

Ribbentrop – 'No one in history has so debauched diplomacy ... he, like the rest of them, is just a common murderer.'

Keitel and Jodl – '[Were they] less involved in murder than their confederates? ... You cannot disguise murder by calling it a political measure.'

Kaltenbrunner – 'As chief of the RSHA, [he] must be guilty ... You will remember his [the witness Hans Gisevius] description of those horrible luncheon parties at which Kaltenbrunner discussed every detail of the gas chambers and of the technique of mass murder.'

Rosenberg – 'His guilt as the philosopher and theorist who made the ground fertile for the seeds of Nazi policy is not in doubt.'

Shawcross then quoted Kaltenbrunner from Nazi reports used in evidence:

'We must annihilate the Jews wherever we find them and whenever it is possible in order to maintain the structure of the Reich as a whole ... We cannot shoot or poison these 3,500,000 Jews, but we shall nevertheless be able to take measures which will lead to their annihilation in some way.'

He went on to say that he was convinced about the guilt of each of the defendants.

'Can Frick, as Minister of Interior, have been unaware of the policy to exterminate the Jews? In 1941 one of his subordinates, Heydrich, was writing to another – the Minister of Justice: "It may safely be assumed that in the future there will be no more Jews in the annexed Eastern Territories." ... Of Streicher, one need say nothing. Here is a man more responsible, perhaps, than any, for the most frightful crime the world has ever known. For 25 years the extermination of the Jews had been his terrible ambition ... It is long since he forfeited all right to live ... That the defendants Schacht and Funk dealt chiefly with economics ought not blind the Tribunal to their important part in the general plan ... Was Dönitz ignorant, when he addressed to a Navy of some 600,000 men, a speech on the "spreading poison of Jewry"? ... Can Raeder have been ignorant of the murder of thousands of Jews at Libau in the Baltic? ...

'What need one say of him [Shirach]? That it were better that a millstone had been placed round his neck? It was this wretched man who perverted millions of innocent German children so that they might grow up and become what they did become – the blind instruments of that policy of murder and domination which these men carried out ... [Papen and Neurath] professed old family and professional integrity – facts which carry with them a great responsibility from which men like Ribbentrop and Kaltenbrunner are free ... As to Seyss-Inquart ... as far as concerns the Jews in the Netherlands, he admits that he knew they were being deported but says he was powerless to stop it as it was ordered from Berlin. He has further said that he knew they went to Auschwitz ... Speer has admitted that his responsibility for conscription of labour helped to bring up the total number of workers under him to 14 million ... [Fritzsche] himself says, in dealing with the uses to which his influence was put: "... again and again I was requested to awaken hatred against individuals and against systems".'

There was no doubting that Shawcross was recommending the severest possible penalty for the guilty parties. Journalists filing their reports noted the stunned expressions on the faces of the defendants. Their fate was now sealed:

> 'Some, it may be, are more guilty than others; some played a more direct and active part than others in these frightful crimes. But when those crimes are such as you have to deal with here ... what mitigation is it that some took less part than others?
>
> 'In one way the fate of these men means little: Their personal power for evil lies forever broken; they have convicted and discredited each other and finally destroyed the legend they created round the figure of their leader. But on their fate great issues must still depend... This Trial must form a milestone in the history of civilization, not only bringing retribution to these guilty men, not only marking that right shall in the end triumph over evil, but also that the ordinary people of the world – and I make no distinction now between friend or foe – are now determined that the individual must transcend the state.'

France and Russia

With Jackson and Shawcross taking the plaudits for their barnstorming final addresses, the efforts of Auguste Champetier de Ribes and General Roman Rudenko were always destined to go unnoticed. Both gave solid, workmanlike performances that thoroughly eschewed the oratorial flourishes of their two colleagues.

Ribes pointed to the historical importance of the trial and the manner in which it had been carried out.

'All the facts have been presented with strict objectivity, leaving no room for passion nor even for sensibility. The Tribunal have excluded from the proceedings everything that, in their opinion, seemed insufficiently proved, everything that might have appeared to be dictated by a spirit of vengeance. For the chief concern of this Trial is above all that of historical truth. Thanks to it, the historian of the future, as well as the chronicler of today, will know the truth of the political, diplomatic, and military events of the most tragic period of our history; he will know the crimes of Nazism as well as the irresolution, the weaknesses, the omissions of the peace-loving democracies. He will know that the work of twenty centuries of a civilization, which believed itself eternal, was almost destroyed by the return of ancient barbarism in a new guise, all the more brutal because more scientific. He will know that the progress of mechanical science, modern means of propaganda, and the most devilish practices of a police which defied the most elementary rules of humanity, enabled a small minority of criminals within a few years to distort the collective conscience of a great people.'

His conclusion was no less scathing than that of Shawcross:

'They must be punished … You must hit hard without pity. It is enough that the verdict be just. To be sure, there are degrees in their guilt. Does it follow that there must be degrees in the penalties themselves, when those whom we consider the least guilty merit the death penalty?'

General Rudenko launched a scathing attack on the defendants and the defence counsel:

> 'Mankind has called the criminals to account and we, the prosecutors, on behalf of all mankind, are the accusers at this Trial. And how pitiful are the efforts to dispute the right of mankind to judge its enemies! How vain the efforts to deprive nations of the right to punish those who made enslavement and genocide their aim, and who for many years strove to realize this criminal aim by criminal methods! ... The defendants, who are accused of the most heinous crimes, are given every possibility to defend themselves ... In their own country the defendants who stood at the helm of the Government destroyed all legal forms of justice, and discarded all the principles of legal procedure accepted by civilized mankind. But they themselves are being tried by an international court with legal guarantees to assure all the rights of defence ... We charge the defendants only with those facts which have been fully established and proved beyond all doubt in the course of the proceedings in which monstrous crimes have been proved, crimes which were prepared over a period of many years by a band of bragging criminals who had seized power in Germany.'

In his conclusion, Rudenko made his demand for punishment absolutely plain:

> 'I consider all the charges against the defendants as fully proven ... I appeal to the Tribunal to sentence all the defendants without exception to the supreme penalty – death. Such a verdict will be greeted with satisfaction by all progressive mankind.'

And so it was that on the morning of 30 July 1946 the cases against the individual defendants at the International Military Tribunal were completed. It was the 191st day of the trial. For the next month, the Tribunal would hear the defence cases for the seven indicted illegal organizations. And the defendants would have four weeks to prepare their final statements before the judges decided on their fate.

The final statements

Under the terms of the London Charter, defendants were permitted to make a final speech to the Tribunal if they chose to do so. In order that all of the statements could be completed in a single day, President Lawrence allowed them each a maximum of 20 minutes' speaking time. At 10 a.m. on 31 August 1946, Hermann Göring entered the witness box once again. He vented his fury that:

> 'The Prosecution, in the final speeches, has treated the defendants and their testimony as completely worthless ... The Prosecution uses the fact that I was the second man of the State as proof that I must have known everything that happened. But it does not present any documentary or other convincing proof in cases where I have denied under oath that I knew about certain things, much less desired them ... Repeatedly we have heard here how the worst crimes were veiled with the most secrecy. I wish to state expressly that I condemn these terrible mass murders to the utmost, and cannot understand them in the least ... I did not want a war, nor did I bring it about. I did everything to prevent it by negotiations ... The only motive which guided me was my ardent love for my people, its happiness, its freedom, and its life. And for this I call on the Almighty and my German people to witness.'

It came as a surprise when Rudolf Hess chose to come to the witness box. He first asked Lawrence if, because of his illness, he could be seated and he then proceeded to read from a five-page statement. It was a barely comprehensible rant mainly aimed at the British government, which took in the Boer War and his apparent deep devotion to God, even though he had 'no spiritual relationship with the Church'. After 20 minutes, Lawrence lost patience and told Hess to conclude his statement.

The leading Nazis are sitting in the dock during the final stages of the trial.

'If I were to begin all over again, I would act just as I have acted, even if I knew that in the end I should meet a fiery death at the stake. No matter what human beings may do, I shall some day stand before the judgment seat of the Eternal. I shall answer to Him, and I know He will judge me innocent.'

Ribbentrop made a brief, obtuse statement in which he read from a telegram he had received from Stalin in 1939, indicating a desire for friendly relations between Germany and the Soviet Union. He concluded that 'the only thing of which I consider myself guilty before my people ... is that my aspirations in foreign policy remained without success.'

Keitel maintained that he'd told the truth throughout his trial, 'even if they incriminated me'. In the end he believed his only mistake was that he had not been 'in a position to prevent what ought to have been prevented. That is my guilt.'

Kaltenbrunner declared that: 'The Prosecution holds me responsible for the concentration camps, for the destruction of Jewish life, for *Einsatzgruppen* and other things. All of this is neither in accord with the evidence nor with the truth.'

He concluded that: 'I am accused here because substitutes are needed for the missing Himmler.'

Rosenberg claimed that: 'Honest service for this ideology, considering all human shortcomings, was not a conspiracy and my actions were never a crime ... I ask you to recognize this as the truth.'

In spite of his declaration during the trial that 'a thousand years would not suffice to erase the guilt brought upon our people because of Hitler's conduct in this war', Frank had an aggressive change of heart:

'Every possible guilt incurred by our nation has already been completely wiped out today, not only by the conduct of our war-time enemies towards our nation and its soldiers ... but also by the tremendous mass crimes of the most frightful sort which – as I have now learned – have been and still are being committed against Germans by Russians, Poles and Czechs, especially in East Prussia, Silesia, Pomerania, and Sudetenland. Who shall ever judge these crimes against the German people?'

Frick gave the briefest of statements, stating that his conscience was clear having spent his whole life

'in the service of my people and my fatherland … I believe that I have deserved punishment no more than have the tens of thousands of faithful German civil servants and officials in the public service who have already been detained in camps for over a year merely because they did their duty.'

Streicher admitted his anti-Semitism, but claimed that in his newspaper, *Der Stürmer*, he had 'advocated the Zionist demand for the creation of a Jewish state as the natural solution of the Jewish problem. These facts prove that I did not want the Jewish problem to be solved by violence.' He claimed that he regretted the mass murders, which could be traced directly to Hitler.

Walther Funk was in tears when he gave his final statement. 'These criminal deeds,' he wept, 'fill me, like every German, with deep shame.' He finally admitted that he had 'let myself be deceived in many things and … I have let myself be deceived all too easily.'

Schacht proclaimed his innocence with the same air of authority he had maintained throughout the trial. He admitted to the error of 'not realizing the extent of Hitler's criminal nature at an early enough time. But,' he concluded, 'I did not stain my hands with one single illegal or immoral act.' As ever, he seemed certain that he would be acquitted.

Having been charged primarily for German submarine warfare, this was the focus of Dönitz's final statement. 'I consider this form of warfare justified and have acted according to my conscience. I would have to do exactly the same all over again.'

As he had done throughout the trial, Raeder continued to portray himself as the obedient military man:

'I have done my duty as a soldier because it was my conviction that this was the best way for me to serve the German people and fatherland, for which I have lived and for which I am prepared to die at any moment. If I have incurred guilt in any way, then this was chiefly in the sense that in spite of my purely military position I should perhaps have been not only a soldier, but also up to a certain point a politician.'

Former Hitler Jugend leader Schirach issued a tearful plea on behalf of the youth of Germany.

'My personal fate is of secondary importance, but youth is the hope of our nation. And if I may express a wish in this last moment, then it is this: Will you, as judges, help to remove the distorted picture of German youth which the world still has today in many places and which cannot stand up under historical investigation? … This Youth has not deserved the hard fate which has come upon it.'

Fritz Sauckel began weeping from the moment of his first words:

'I have been shaken to the very depths of my soul by the atrocities revealed in this Trial. In all humility and reverence, I bow before the victims and the fallen of all nations, and before the misfortune and suffering of my own people, with whom alone I must measure my fate … I only became a National Socialist because I condemned class struggle, expropriation, and civil war, and because I firmly believed in Hitler's absolute desire for peace and understanding with the rest of the world.'

Alfred Jodl believed that history would vindicate the defendants on trial in the sure knowledge that Hitler was the one true villain:

'For they, and the entire German Wehrmacht with them, were confronted with an insoluble task, namely, to conduct a war which they had not wanted; under a commander-in-chief whose confidence they did not possess and whom they themselves only trusted within limits ... And all this in the complete and clear realization that this war would decide the life or death of our beloved fatherland. They did not serve the powers of Hell and they did not serve a criminal, but rather their people and their fatherland.'

Franz von Papen believed he had always acted in the interests of Germany and that he had co-operated with the Nazis

'by occupying a prominent position ... because I considered it to be my duty, because I believed in the possibility of steering National Socialism into responsible channels, and because I hoped that the maintenance of Christian principles would be the best counterweight against ideological and political radicalism and would guarantee peaceful domestic and foreign development ... When I examine my conscience, I do not find any guilt where the Prosecution has looked for it and claims to have found it.'

To the very end, Arthur Seyss-Inquart remained loyal to Hitler:

'To me he remains the man who made Greater Germany a fact in German history. I served this man. And now? I cannot today cry "Crucify him", since yesterday I cried "Hosanna" ... My last word is the principle by which I have always acted and to which I will adhere to my last breath: "I believe in Germany".'

In his final statement, Albert Speer made no personal plea but instead gave a curious but prescient warning of the dangers posed by technological advancement on future weapons. He foresaw a world where:

'In five or ten years … it [will be] possible to fire rockets from continent to continent with uncanny precision. By atomic power it can destroy one million people in the centre of New York in a matter of seconds with a rocket operated, perhaps, by only ten men, invisible, without previous warning, faster than sound, by day and by night. Science is able to spread pestilence among human beings and animals and to destroy crops by insect warfare. Chemistry has developed terrible weapons with which it can inflict unspeakable suffering upon helpless human beings … A new large-scale war will end with the destruction of human culture and civilization.'

Konstantin von Neurath spoke for just 30 seconds. His conscience was clear, he said:

'If, in spite of this, the Tribunal should find me guilty, I shall be able to bear even this and take it upon myself as a last sacrifice on behalf of my people, to serve whom was the substance and purpose of my life.'

Hans Fritzsche, for his part, claimed merely to have been misled. 'I believed in Hitler's assurances of a sincere desire for peace,' he claimed. 'I believed in the official German denials of all foreign reports of German atrocities … That is my guilt – no more, no less.'

And with that, Geoffrey Lawrence made his final pronouncement of the day: 'The Tribunal will carefully consider the statements which the defendants have made … The Tribunal will now adjourn until 23 September, in order to consider its judgment. On that date the judgment will be announced.'

It would be Monday, 30 September before the Tribunal next met.

The Endgame

On the morning of Tuesday, 1 October 1946, almost 11 months after the Nuremberg Trials had begun, Tribunal President Colonel Sir Geoffrey Lawrence began the process of passing judgement on the defendants – a task that was shared among the Allied judges throughout the morning. The charges would be based on the four indictment counts read out on the first day of the trial of the major Nazi war criminals on 20 November 1945: 'One: Common Plan or Conspiracy; Two: Crimes Against Peace; Three: War Crimes; Four: Crimes Against Humanity.'

The sentencing took place in the afternoon, following the lunchtime recess.

Hermann Göring (Indicted on all four counts)*:*

'The evidence shows that after Hitler he was the most prominent man in the Nazi regime ... He testified that Hitler kept him informed of all important military and political problems ... Goering attended the Reich Chancellery meeting of 23 May 1939, when Hitler told his military leaders "there is, therefore, no question of sparing Poland" ... He commanded the Luftwaffe in the attack on Poland and throughout the aggressive wars which followed ... there can remain no doubt that Goering was the moving force for aggressive war second only to Hitler. He was the planner and prime mover in the military and diplomatic preparation for war which Germany pursued ... Goering was the active authority in the spoliation of conquered territory. He

Tribunal President Colonel Sir Geoffrey Lawrence reads part of the final verdicts at the end of the war crimes trials in Nuremberg on 30 September 1946.

made plans for the spoliation of Soviet territory long before the war on the Soviet Union ... His own admissions are more than sufficiently wide to be conclusive of his guilt. His guilt is unique in its enormity. The record discloses no excuses for this man.'

'The Tribunal finds the Defendant Goering guilty on all four counts of the Indictment.'

Rudolf Hess (Indicted on all four counts):

'He joined the Nazi Party in 1920 and participated in the Munich Putsch on 9 November 1923. He was imprisoned with Hitler in the Landsberg fortress ... and became Hitler's closest personal confidant ... As Deputy to the Fuehrer, Hess was the top man in the Nazi Party with responsibility for handling all Party matters and authority to make decisions in Hitler's name on all questions of Party leadership.

'It is true that between 1933 and 1937 Hess made speeches in which he expressed a desire for peace and advocated international economic co-operation. But nothing which they contained can alter the fact that of all the defendants none knew better than Hess how determined Hitler was to realize his ambitions, how fanatical and violent a man he was, and how little likely he was to refrain from resorting to force if this was the only way in which he could achieve his aims.

'That Hess acts in an abnormal manner, suffers from loss of memory, and has mentally deteriorated during this Trial, may be true. But there is nothing to show that he does not realize the nature of the charges against him, or is incapable of defending himself. He was ably represented at the Trial by counsel, appointed for that purpose by the Tribunal. There is no suggestion that Hess was not completely sane when the acts charged against him were committed.'

'The Tribunal finds the Defendant Hess guilty on counts one and two; and not guilty on counts three and four.'

Joachim von Ribbentrop (Indicted on all four counts):

'When Ribbentrop became Foreign Minister, Hitler told him that Germany still had four problems to solve: Austria, Sudetenland, Memel, and Danzig, and mentioned the possibility of ... "military settlement" for their solution ... he participated in the aggressive plans against Czechoslovakia ... was instrumental in inducing the Slovaks to proclaim their independence ... Ribbentrop was advised in advance of the attack on Norway and Denmark and of the attack on the Low Countries and prepared the official Foreign Office memoranda attempting to justify these aggressive actions.

'He played an important part in Hitler's "final solution" of the Jewish question. In September 1942 he ordered the German diplomatic representatives accredited to various Axis satellites to hasten the deportation of Jews to the East.

'Although he was personally concerned with the diplomatic rather than the military aspect of these actions, his diplomatic efforts were so closely connected with war that he could not have remained unaware of the aggressive nature of Hitler's actions ... His collaboration with Hitler and with other defendants in the commission of Crimes against Peace, War Crimes and Crimes against Humanity was whole-hearted.'

'The Tribunal finds that Ribbentrop is guilty on all four counts.'

Wilhelm Keitel (Indicted on all four counts):

'Present on 23 May 1939 when Hitler announced his decision "to attack Poland at the first suitable opportunity" ... [he] ordered that attacks on soldiers in the East should be met by putting to death 50 to 100 Communists for one German soldier – with the comment that human life was less than nothing in the East ... He ordered military commanders always to have hostages to execute when German soldiers were attacked ... [He] directed that Russian prisoners of war be used in German war industry ... He was present on 4 January 1944 when Hitler directed Sauckel to obtain 4 million new workers from occupied territories.

'Superior orders, even to a soldier, cannot be considered in mitigation where crimes so shocking and extensive have been committed consciously, ruthlessly, and without military excuse or justification.'

'The Tribunal finds Keitel guilty on all four counts.'

Ernst Kaltenbrunner (Indicted on counts one, three and four):

'When he became Chief of the Security Police and SD [Nazi intelligence service] and head of the RSHA [Reich Main Security Office] on 30 January 1943, Kaltenbrunner took charge of an organization which included the main offices of the Gestapo, the SD, and the Criminal Police. As Chief of the RSHA, Kaltenbrunner had authority to order protective custody to, and release from, concentration camps ... Kaltenbrunner was aware of conditions in concentration camps ... witnesses testified that he had seen prisoners killed by the various methods of execution, hanging, shooting in the back of the neck, and gassing, as part of a demonstration ... Kaltenbrunner himself ordered the execution of prisoners in those camps ... At the end of the war Kaltenbrunner participated in the arrangements for the evacuation of inmates of concentration camps, and the liquidation of many of them, to prevent them from being liberated by the Allied armies.

'The RSHA played a leading part in the "final solution" of the Jewish question by the extermination of the Jews ... Under its direction approximately 6 million Jews were murdered ... [and] approximately 4 million Jews [were murdered] in concentration camps ... under the supervision of the RSHA ... He claims that the criminal program had been started before his assumption of office; that he seldom knew what was going on; and that when he was informed he did what he could to stop them ... But he exercised control over the activities of the RSHA, was aware of the crimes it was committing, and was an active participant in many of them.'

'The Tribunal finds that Kaltenbrunner is not guilty on count one. He is guilty under counts three and four.'

Alfred Rosenberg (Indicted on all four counts):

'Recognized as the Party's ideologist ... His book *Myth of the Twentieth Century* had a circulation of over a million copies ... Rosenberg, together with Raeder, was one of the originators of the plan for attacking Norway ... Rosenberg bears a major responsibility for the formulation and execution of occupation policies in the Occupied Eastern Territories ... Rosenberg is responsible for a system of organized plunder of both public and private property throughout the invaded countries of Europe ... With his appointment as Reich Minister for the Occupied Eastern Territories, Rosenberg became the supreme authority for those areas. He helped to formulate the policies of Germanization, exploitation, forced labour, extermination of Jews and opponents of Nazi rule, and he set up the administration which carried them out ... [and] took an active part in stripping the Eastern territories of raw materials and foodstuffs, which were sent to Germany. He stated that feeding the German people was first on the list of claims on the East, and that the Soviet people would suffer thereby.'

'*The Tribunal finds that Rosenberg is guilty on all four counts.*'

Hans Frank (Indicted under counts one, three and four):

'Governor General of the occupied Polish territory ... he described the policy which he intended to put into effect by stating: "Poland shall be treated like a colony; the Poles will become the slaves of the Greater German World Empire" ... [the policy was based on] the complete destruction of Poland as a national entity, and a ruthless exploitation of its human and economic resources for the German war effort ... The concentration camp system was introduced by the Governor General by the establishment of the notorious Treblinka and Majdanek camps …

'Frank introduced the deportation of slave labourers to Germany in the very early stages of his administration … he indicated his intention of deporting a million labourers to Germany, suggesting … "the use of police raids to meet this quota."

'Frank was a willing and knowing participant in the use of terrorism in Poland; in the economic exploitation of Poland in a way which led to the death by starvation of a large number of people; in the deportation to Germany as slave labourers of over a million Poles; and in a program involving the murder of at least 3 million Jews.'

'The Tribunal finds that Frank is not guilty on count one but is guilty under counts three and four.'

Wilhelm Frick (Indicted on all four counts):

'An avid Nazi, Frick was largely responsible for bringing the German nation under the complete control of the NSDAP [Nazi Party]. After Hitler became Reich Chancellor, the new Minister of the Interior immediately began to incorporate local governments under the sovereignty of the Reich … [he] abolished all opposition parties and prepared the way for the Gestapo and their concentration camps to extinguish all individual opposition. He was largely responsible for the legislation which suppressed the trade unions, the Church, the Jews. He performed this task with ruthless efficiency.

'Rabidly anti-Semitic, Frick drafted, signed, and administered many laws designed to eliminate Jews from German life and economy. His work formed the basis of the Nuremberg Decrees, and he was active in enforcing them. [He was] Responsible for prohibiting Jews from following various professions.

'As the supreme Reich authority in Bohemia and Moravia, Frick bears general responsibility for the acts of oppression in that territory ... such as terrorism of the population, slave labour, and the deportation of Jews to the concentration camps for extermination ... He had knowledge that insane, sick, and aged people ... were being systematically put to death. Complaints of these murders reached him but he did nothing to stop them.'

'The Tribunal finds that Frick is not guilty on count one. He is guilty on counts two, three and four.'

Julius Streicher (Indicted on counts one and four):

'One of the earliest members of the Nazi Party ... His persecution of the Jews was notorious. He was the publisher of *Der Stürmer*, an anti-Semitic weekly newspaper ... Streicher was a staunch Nazi and supporter of Hitler's main policies. There is no evidence to show that he was ever within Hitler's inner circle of advisers; nor during his career was he closely connected with the formulation of the policies which led to war ... For his 25 years of speaking, writing, and preaching hatred of the Jews, Streicher was widely known as "Jew-Baiter Number One". In his speeches and articles, week after week, month after month, he infected the German mind with the virus of anti-Semitism and incited the German people to active persecution ... But the evidence makes it clear that he continually received current information on the progress of the "final solution".

'Streicher's incitement to murder and extermination at the time when Jews in the East were being killed under the most horrible conditions clearly constitutes persecution on political and racial grounds in connection with War Crimes, as defined by the Charter, and constitutes a Crime against Humanity.'

'The Tribunal finds that Streicher is not guilty on count one, but that he is guilty on count four.'

Walther Funk (Indicted on all four counts):

'Funk became active in the economic field after the Nazi plans to wage aggressive war had been clearly defined ... On 25 August 1939, Funk wrote a letter to Hitler expressing his gratitude that he was able to participate in such world-shaking events; that his plans for the "financing of the war", for the control of wage and price conditions and for the strengthening of the Reichsbank had been completed; and that he had inconspicuously transferred into gold all foreign exchange resources available to Germany ... Funk was not one of the leading figures in originating the Nazi plans for aggressive war ... He did, however, participate in the economic preparation for certain of the aggressive wars, notably those against Poland and the Soviet Union ... [He] had participated in the early Nazi program of economic discrimination against the Jews ... he attended a meeting held under the chairmanship of Göring to discuss the solution of the Jewish problem and proposed a decree providing for the banning of Jews from all business activities, which Göring issued the same day ...

'[The] SS sent to the Reichsbank the personal belongings taken from the victims who had been exterminated in the concentration camps. The Reichsbank kept the coins and bank notes and sent the jewels, watches, and personal belongings to Berlin municipal pawn shops. The gold from the eyeglasses and gold teeth and fillings were stored in the Reichsbank vaults ... As Minister of Economics and President of the Reichsbank, Funk participated in the economic exploitation of occupied territories ... He was responsible for the seizure of the gold reserves of the Czechoslovakian National Bank and for the liquidation of the Yugoslavian National Bank ... As President of the Reichsbank, Funk was also indirectly involved in the utilization of concentration camp labour ... '

'Funk was never a dominant figure in the various programs in which he participated. This is a mitigating fact of which the Tribunal takes notice. The Tribunal finds that Funk is not guilty on count one but is guilty under counts two, three, and four ... '

Hjalmar Schacht (Indicted on counts one and two):

'Schacht was an active supporter of the Nazi Party before its accession to power ... and supported the appointment of Hitler to the post of Chancellor. After that date he played an important role in the vigorous rearmament program which was adopted, using the facilities of the Reichsbank to the fullest extent in the German rearmament effort ... He was clearly not one of the inner circle around Hitler which was most closely involved with this common plan – he was regarded by this group with undisguised hostility.'

'The Tribunal finds that Schacht is not guilty ... and directs that he shall be discharged by the Marshal when the Tribunal presently adjourns.'

Karl Dönitz (Indicted on counts one, two and three):

'Although Dönitz built and trained the German U-Boat arm, the evidence does not show he was privy to the conspiracy to wage aggressive wars or that he prepared and initiated such wars ... Dönitz is charged with waging unrestricted submarine warfare contrary to the Naval Protocol of 1936, to which Germany acceded ... The German U-Boat arm began to wage unrestricted submarine warfare upon all merchant ships, whether enemy or neutral, cynically disregarding the Protocol ...

'The Prosecution has introduced much evidence surrounding two orders of Dönitz, War Order Number 154, issued in 1939, and the so-called Laconia order of 1942. The Defense argues that these orders and the evidence supporting them do not show such a policy and introduced much evidence to the contrary. The Tribunal is of the opinion that the evidence does not establish with the certainty required that Dönitz deliberately ordered the killing of shipwrecked survivors. The orders were undoubtedly ambiguous, and deserve the strongest censure.'

'The Tribunal finds Dönitz is not guilty on count one of the indictment, and is guilty on counts two and three.'

Erich Raeder (Indicted on counts one, two and three):

'In the 15 years he commanded it, Raeder built and directed the German Navy; he accepts full responsibility until retirement in 1943. He admits the Navy violated the Versailles Treaty, insisting it was "a matter of honour for every man" to do so. The conception of the invasion of Norway first arose in the mind of Raeder and not that of Hitler ... Germany's invasion of Norway and Denmark was aggressive war ...

'Raeder endeavoured to dissuade Hitler from embarking upon the invasion of the U.S.S.R. In September 1940 he urged on Hitler an aggressive Mediterranean policy as an alternative to an attack on Russia. On 14 November 1940 he urged the war against England "as our main enemy" and that submarine and naval air force construction be continued ... It is clear from this evidence that Raeder participated in the planning and waging of aggressive war ...

'Raeder is charged with war crimes on the high seas. The *Athenia*, an unarmed British passenger liner, was sunk on 3 September 1939, while outward bound to America. The Germans two months later charged that Mr. Churchill deliberately sank the *Athenia* to encourage American hostility to Germany. In fact, it was sunk by the German U-Boat U-30 ...The most serious charge against Raeder is that he carried out unrestricted submarine warfare, including sinking of unarmed merchant ships, of neutrals, non-rescue and machine-gunning of survivors, contrary to the London Protocol of 1936..."

'The Tribunal finds that Raeder is guilty on counts one, two and three.'

Baldur von Schirach (Indicted under counts one and four):

'In 1931 he was made Reich Youth Leader of the Nazi Party with control over all Nazi youth organizations including the Hitler Jugend ... After the Nazis had come to power, Von Schirach, utilizing both physical violence and official pressure, either drove out of existence or took over all youth groups which competed with the Hitler Jugend ... Von Schirach used the Hitler Jugend to educate German youth "in the spirit of National Socialism" and subjected them to an intensive program of Nazi propaganda ... Von Schirach also used the Hitler Jugend for premilitary training ... The Hitler Jugend placed particular emphasis on the military spirit, and its training program stressed the importance of return of the colonies, the necessity for *Lebensraum*, and the noble destiny of German youth to die for Hitler...

'When Von Schirach became Gauleiter of Vienna the deportation of the Jews had already begun, and only 60,000 out of Vienna's original 190,000 Jews remained. On 2 October 1940, he attended a conference at Hitler's office and told Frank that he had 50,000 Jews in Vienna which the Government General would have to take over from him ... On 15 September 1942, Von Schirach made a speech in which he defended his action in having "tens of thousands upon tens of thousands of Jews into the ghetto of the East" as "contributing to European culture" ...

'The Tribunal finds that Von Schirach, while he did not originate the policy of deporting Jews from Vienna, participated in this deportation after he had become Gauleiter of Vienna. He knew that the best the Jews could hope for was a miserable existence in the ghettos of the East. Bulletins describing the Jewish extermination were in his office.'

'The Tribunal finds that Von Schirach is not guilty on count one. He is guilty under count four.'

Fritz Sauckel (Indicted on all four counts):

'The evidence has not satisfied the Tribunal that Sauckel was sufficiently connected with the common plan to wage aggressive war or sufficiently involved in the planning or waging of the aggressive wars to allow the Tribunal to convict him on counts one or two ...

'Sauckel set up a program for the mobilization of the labour resources available to the Reich ... the systematic exploitation, by force, of the labour resources of the occupied territories ... He described so-called "voluntary" recruiting by "a whole batch of male and female agents just as was done in the olden times for shanghaiing." That real voluntary recruiting was the exception rather than the rule is shown by Sauckel's statement on 1 March 1944, that "out of five million foreign workers who arrived in Germany not even 200,000 came voluntarily."

'Sauckel had overall responsibility for the slave labour program ... He was aware of ruthless methods being taken to obtain labourers and vigorously supported them on the ground that they were necessary to fill the quotas. It does not appear that he advocated brutality for its own sake, or was an advocate of any program such as Himmler's plan for extermination through work ... The evidence shows that Sauckel was in charge of a program which involved deportation for slave labour of more than 5 million human beings, many of them under terrible conditions of cruelty and suffering.'

'The Tribunal finds that Sauckel is not guilty on counts one and two. He is guilty under counts three and four.'

Alfred Jodl (Indicted on all four counts):

'In the strict military sense, Jodl was the actual planner of the war and responsible in large measure for the strategy and conduct of operations ... [He] defends himself on the ground he was a soldier sworn to obedience, and not a politician ... Though he claims that as a soldier he had to obey Hitler, he says that he often tried to obstruct certain measures by delay, which occasionally proved successful ...

'In planning the attack on Czechoslovakia, Jodl was very active ... The genius of the Führer and his determination not to shun even a world war have again won the victory without the use of force. The hope remains that the incredulous, the weak, and the doubtful people have been converted and will remain that way ... He was active in the planning against Greece and Yugoslavia ... Jodl testified that Hitler feared an attack by Russia and so attacked first. This preparation began almost a year before the invasion ... Jodl ordered the evacuation of all persons in northern Norway and the burning of their houses so they could not help the Russians ... On 7 October 1941, Jodl signed an order that Hitler would not accept an offer of surrender of Leningrad or Moscow, but on the contrary he insisted that they be completely destroyed ... '

'There is nothing in mitigation. Participation in such crimes as these has never been required of any soldier and he cannot now shield himself behind a mythical requirement of soldierly obedience ... The Tribunal finds that Jodl is guilty on all four counts.'

Franz von Papen (Indicted on counts one and two):

'Von Papen was active in 1932 and 1933 in helping Hitler to form the Coalition Cabinet and aided in his appointment as Chancellor on 30 January 1933. As Vice Chancellor in that

Cabinet he participated in the Nazi consolidation of control in 1933. On 16 June 1934, however, Von Papen made a speech at Marburg which contained a denunciation of the Nazi attempts to suppress the free press and the Church, of the existence of a reign of terror, and of "150 percent Nazis" who were mistaking "brutality for vitality" …

'As Minister to Austria, Von Papen was active in trying to strengthen the position of the Nazi Party in Austria for the purpose of bringing about the *Anschluss* … No evidence has been offered showing that Von Papen was in favour of the decision to occupy Austria by force, and he has testified that he urged Hitler not to take this step … After the annexation of Austria Von Papen retired into private life and there is no evidence that he took any part in politics … '

'The Tribunal finds that Von Papen is not guilty under this indictment and directs that he shall be discharged by the Marshal, when the Tribunal presently adjourns.'

Arthur Seyss-Inquart (Indicted under all four counts):

'Seyss-Inquart participated in the last stages of the Nazi "intrigue" which preceded the German occupation of Austria and was made Chancellor of Austria as a result of German threats of invasion … As Reich Governor of Austria, Seyss-Inquart instituted a program of confiscating Jewish property … Jews were forced to emigrate, were sent to concentration camps, and were subject to pogroms … While he was Governor of Austria, political opponents of the Nazis were sent to concentration camps by the Gestapo, mistreated, and often killed …

'As Deputy Governor General of the Government General of Poland, Seyss-Inquart was a supporter of the harsh occupation policies which were put in effect … [He] also advocated the persecution of Jews …

'As Reich Commissioner for Occupied Netherlands, Seyss-Inquart was ruthless in applying terrorism to suppress all opposition to the German occupation, a program which he described as "annihilating" his opponents ... A policy was adopted for the maximum utilization of the economic potential of the Netherlands, and executed with small regard for its effect on the inhabitants. There was widespread pillage of public and private property ... During the occupation over 500,000 people were sent from the Netherlands to the Reich as labourers, and only a very small proportion were actually volunteers ... [Regarding] the mass deportation of almost 120,000 of Holland's 140,000 Jews to Auschwitz and the "final solution". [He] admits knowing that they were going to Auschwitz but ... thought that they were being held there for resettlement after the war. In the light of the evidence and on account of his official position it is impossible to believe this claim ...'

The Tribunal finds that Seyss-Inquart is guilty under counts two, three, and four; Seyss-Inquart is not guilty on count one.'

Albert Speer (Indicted on all four counts):

'The Tribunal is of the opinion that Speer's activities do not amount to initiating, planning, or preparing wars of aggression, or of conspiring to that end ... The evidence introduced against Speer under counts three and four relates entirely to his participation in the slave labour program. As Reich Minister for Armaments and Munitions ... Speer had extensive authority over production ... As the dominant member of the Central Planning Board, which had supreme authority for the scheduling of German production and the allocation and development of raw materials, Speer took the position that the board had authority to instruct Sauckel to provide labourers for industries under its control ... Speer knew when he made his demands on Sauckel that they would be supplied by foreign labourers serving under compulsion ... [He] attended a conference in Hitler's headquarters on 4 January 1944, at which the decision was made that Sauckel should obtain "at least four million new workers from occupied territories' in order to satisfy the demands for labour made by Speer ...

'Speer's position was such that he was not directly concerned with the cruelty in the administration of the slave labour program, although he was aware of its existence ... In mitigation it must be recognized that Speer's establishment of blocked industries did keep many labourers in their homes and that in the closing stages of the war he was one of the few men who had the courage to tell Hitler that the war was lost and to take steps to prevent the senseless destruction of production facilities, both in occupied territories and in Germany ... '

'The Tribunal finds that Speer is not guilty on counts one and two, but is guilty under counts three and four.'

Konstantin von Neurath (Indicted on all four counts):

'As Minister of Foreign Affairs, Von Neurath advised Hitler in connection with the withdrawal from the Disarmament Conference and the League of Nations [in 1933] ... [He] played an important part in Hitler's decision to reoccupy the Rhineland [in 1936] ...

'Von Neurath was appointed Reich Protector for Bohemia and Moravia [which] were occupied by military force ... [and] must therefore be considered a military occupation covered by the rules of warfare ... Free press, political parties, and trade unions were abolished. All groups which might serve as opposition were outlawed. Czechoslovakian industry was worked into the structure of German war production, and exploited for the German war effort. Nazi anti-Semitic policies and laws were also introduced. Jews were barred from leading positions in government and business ...

'When the war broke out ... 8,000 prominent Czechs were arrested by the Security Police ... and put into protective custody. Many of this group died in concentration camps as a result of mistreatment ... He served as the chief German official in the Protectorate when the administration of this territory played an important role in the wars of aggression which Germany was waging in the East, knowing that war crimes and crimes against humanity were being committed under his authority ...'

'The Tribunal finds that Von Neurath is guilty under all four counts.'

Hans Fritzsche (Indicted on counts one, three, and four):

'He was best known as a radio commentator, discussing once a week the events of the day on his own program, "Hans Fritzsche Speaks." In November 1942 [he was] made head of the Radio Division of the Propaganda Ministry ... As head of the Home Press Division, Fritzsche supervised the German press of 2,300 daily newspapers. In pursuance of this function he held daily press conferences to deliver the directives of the Propaganda Ministry to these papers ... these instructions ... directed the press to present to the people certain themes, such as the leadership principle, the Jewish problem, the problem of living space, or other standard Nazi ideas. A vigorous propaganda campaign was carried out before each major act of aggression ... he instructed the press how the actions or wars against Bohemia and Moravia, Poland, Yugoslavia, and the Soviet Union should be dealt with ... [He] was present at Goebbels' daily staff conferences. Here they were instructed in the news and propaganda policies of the day ...

'The Tribunal is not prepared to hold that [his broadcasts] were intended to incite the German people to commit atrocities on conquered peoples, and he cannot be held to have been a participant in the crimes charged. His aim was rather to arouse popular sentiment in support of Hitler and the German war effort.'

'The Tribunal finds that Fritzsche is not guilty under this indictment, and directs that he shall be discharged by the Marshal when the Tribunal presently adjourns.'

Martin Bormann (Indicted on counts one, three, and four):

'Bormann, in the beginning a minor Nazi, steadily rose to a position of power and, particularly in the closing days, of great influence over Hitler. He was active in the Party's rise to power and even more so in the consolidation of that power...

'Bormann was extremely active in the persecution of the Jews not only in Germany but also in the absorbed or conquered countries. He took part in the discussions which led to the removal of 60,000 Jews from Vienna to Poland ... he [extended] the Nuremberg Laws to the annexed Eastern territories ... [In] October 1942 he declared that the permanent elimination of Jews in Greater German territory could no longer be solved by emigration, but only by applying "ruthless force" in the special camps in the East ...

'Bormann was prominent in the slave labour program ... A report of 4 September 1942 relating to the transfer of 500,000 female domestic workers from the East to Germany showed that control was to be exercised by Sauckel, Himmler, and Bormann ...

'Counsel has argued that Bormann is dead ... but the evidence of death is not conclusive, and the Tribunal, as previously stated, determined to try him *in absentia*. If Bormann is not dead and is later apprehended, the Control Council for Germany may, under Article 29 of the Charter, consider any facts in mitigation, and alter or reduce his sentence, if deemed proper.'

'The Tribunal finds that Bormann is not guilty on count one, but is guilty on counts three and four.'

The sentencing

After the lunch recess, the atmosphere in the courtroom altered. The Tribunal had demanded that each man facing his sentence – death or long imprisonment – would be afforded the respect of a solemn courtroom. No photographers or filming would be allowed, so the ambient lighting was lower than had been normal. One at a time, each defendant would enter the courtroom, his sentence would be read out, and he would leave. First to enter the room was Göring, exhibiting the same studied indifference that had accompanied much of the past year in the courtroom. After a farcical start in which Göring's headphones malfunctioned, Lawrence made his first pronouncement of the afternoon.

'Defendant Hermann Wilhelm Goering, on the Counts of the Indictment on which you have been convicted, the International Military Tribunal sentences you to death by hanging.'

No expression crossed Göring's face. It was, after all, what he had expected from the beginning. He turned and left. Once out of the lift, like all of the convicted prisoners now, he was handcuffed to a guard during the walk back to his cell.

Next up was Rudolf Hess. By this time in the proceedings Hess seemed genuinely deranged. Nobody had known for sure how much of this was an act, but as he stood there, swaying in the dock, a crazed expression on his face, it was hard not to believe that he wasn't entirely present.

'Defendant Rudolf Hess, on the Counts of the Indictment on which you have been convicted, the Tribunal sentences you to imprisonment for life.'

He seemed not to notice what was happening until one of the US military guards tapped his shoulder and pointed to the lift. Like Göring, Ribbentrop, Keitel, Kaltenbrunner, Frank and Frick barely needed to be told of their fates – Lawrence solemnly pronounced 'death by hanging' each time. Kaltenbrunner, who had bowed politely as he entered, bowed once more as he left. Frank breathed a silent 'thank you' as he made his final exit.

Streicher, the obnoxious, rabble-rousing newspaper man, loathed by almost everyone with whom he'd come into contact at Nuremberg, reacted to his verdict – also 'death by hanging' – with anger and stormed off to the door of the lift.

Within the hour, all of the sentences had been handed out: Sauckel, Jodl and Seyss-Inquart, 'death by hanging'; Funk and Raeder, 'imprisonment for life'; Schirach and Speer, 'twenty years' imprisonment'; Neurath, 'fifteen years' imprisonment'; Dönitz, 'ten years' imprisonment'.

Although tried *in absentia*, Martin Bormann was also sentenced to death by hanging. The truth about Bormann's fate would be debated for many years. In 1964, the West German government offered a reward of 100,000 Deutsche Marks for information leading to his capture. Celebrated Nazi hunter Simon Wiesenthal believed that, like other prominent Nazis, he had fled to South America, while a book written by a former Nazi intelligence officer claimed he had been a Soviet spy and had escaped to Moscow. There were also sightings of him across the globe from Denmark to Australia. The story believed by most came from Hitler Youth leader Artur Axmann, who said that following the deaths of Hitler and Goebbels, Bormann had left the Führerbunker on 2 May 1945 and had been killed during the Red Army shelling of Berlin. Axmann claimed to have seen Bormann's body, along with that of SS doctor Ludwig Stumpfegger, on a nearby railway bridge. Then in 1963 a retired postal worker told the police that around that time Soviet troops had ordered him to bury two bodies near the bridge. Although excavations produced nothing, nine years later builders working nearby discovered two skeletons. Dental and medical records showed one of them to be Bormann. He had indeed perished just two days after his beloved Führer.

Before the Tribunal finally adjourned, there was time for one last minor legal row, as 'the Soviet member of the International Military Tribunal desires to record his dissent from the decisions in the cases of the defendants Schacht, von Papen, and Fritzsche. He is of the opinion that they should have been convicted and not acquitted.' He also wanted it recorded that Hess should have been executed rather than be sentenced to life in prison. And as far as the Tribunal was concerned, that was that.

The denouement

Nuremberg was in the American occupied zone, so the US military was tasked with carrying out the 11 executions; they were scheduled to take place in the prison gymnasium early on 16 October 1946. There was yet time for one final drama to unfold. Shortly after lights-out on the night of 15 October there was a disturbance in one of the prison cells. Although Göring's guard thought he was merely sleeping, he began twitching violently, followed by convulsions and frothing around the lips. By the time the prison doctor arrived, Göring was dead. It seemed like a well-timed heart attack, until closer inspection revealed tiny shards of glass in his mouth. Göring had bitten on a cyanide phial and taken his own life. Furious, the Allied authorities ordered all prison staff to be interviewed: nobody truly believed that he could have kept cyanide secreted about his person during more than a year of captivity. Prison psychologist Gustave Gilbert, who had been something of a confidant to Göring during his time at Nuremberg, described him in his diary as an 'amiable psychopath'. But for this act he regarded him as a coward, 'for he died as he had lived, a psychopath trying to make a mockery of all human values and to detract from his guilt by a dramatic gesture'.

At 11 minutes past one, in the early hours of 16 October 1946, Joachim von Ribbentrop was brought from his cell. One at a time, each prisoner was to stand beneath the gallows. Then his handcuffs would be released and replaced with a black cord, his feet would be tethered with a belt and a black hood would be placed over his head – followed by the noose. One of the two hangmen – Master Sergeant John C. Woods and military policeman Joseph Malta – would pull the lever and the prisoner would drop. With the exception of Göring, that is, who had managed to cheat the hangman.

Each condemned man was given the opportunity to say his last words. The *Manchester Guardian* newspaper reported the event in some detail: 'Not one of them broke down,' it reported. 'God protect Germany!' Ribbentrop declared: 'My last wish is that German unity should remain

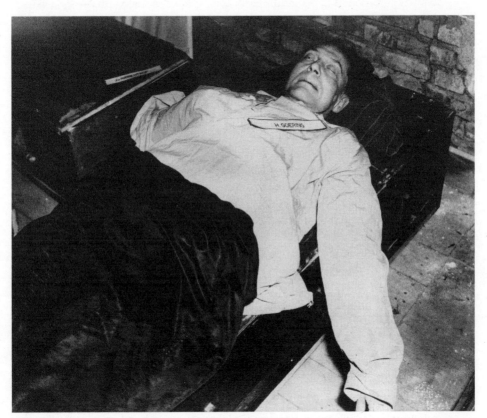

The corpse of Hermann Göring, who committed suicide before his sentence of execution could be carried out.

and that an understanding between the East and West will come about and peace for the world.'

Julius Streicher went to his death characteristically railing at his enemies, shouting 'Heil Hitler!' The newspaper went on to report that: 'as he was led up the steps, he shouted from the top of the scaffold: "The Bolsheviks will hang you all next Jewish holiday! Jewish holiday, 1946! Now it goes to God."' Kaltenbrunner was somewhat more philosophical: 'I have loved my German people and my Fatherland from the bottom of my heart. I have done my duty by the laws of my country. I regret that my people were not led by soldiers only and that crimes were committed in which I had no share. I fought honourably. Germany – good luck.'

Seyss-Inquart quietly declared: 'I hope this execution will be the last act in the tragedy of a second world war and that its lessons will be learned, so that peace and understanding will follow … I believe in Germany.'

The gruesome operation took one hour and 34 minutes. Although the bodies were at first rumoured to have been taken to Dachau concentration camp for incineration, it was later confirmed that they had been transported to a crematorium in Munich and the ashes scattered on the River Isar.

The 'free' men

Acquittal at Nuremberg was a bittersweet pill for some of the defendants. Most agreed that Fritzsche was a minor figure who had only been tried because Goebbels had escaped justice by taking his own life. He was nonetheless tried by a West German 'denazification' court in 1947 and sent to prison, dying in 1950. A similar fate befell Franz von Papen, who received an eight-year sentence but was released on appeal after two years. He died in 1969 at the age of 89. Only Dr Hjalmar Schacht was able to resume a normal post-Nuremberg existence. He started a bank in 1953 which he led for ten years, and lived the life of a wealthy, successful businessman until 1970, when he died at the age of 93.

The prisoners

Those who escaped the hangman's noose spent the majority of their remaining years in Spandau Prison in West Berlin. Funk's life sentence was terminated in 1957 when he was released because of ill health. He died three years later. Neurath was released in 1954 after suffering a heart attack; he died within 18 months. Raeder was also released for health reasons and died in 1960. Schirach served his full 20-year sentence and was released in 1966 after which he retired to Bavaria to publish his memoirs. He died in 1974. Dönitz did much the same. After serving his ten-year sentence he retired to rural Schleswig-Holstein until his death in 1980.

Albert Speer became something of a celebrity during his time at Spandau. His release in 1966 was a major media event and he devoted much of the remainder of his life to revisionism. Through his books and numerous interviews and media appearances he tried to cast himself as the 'good Nazi', the technocrat unaware of the atrocities going on around him. He died in 1981.

In spite of his suicide attempts while a British prisoner of war, not to mention his mental health problems throughout the trial of major Nazi war criminals at Nuremberg, Rudolf Hess lived to the grand age of 93, when he made his final, successful suicide bid, hanging himself with an electric cable. Although Spandau Prison had been built in the 1870s to hold up to 600 inmates, after the war it housed only the Nuremberg prisoners – the 'Spandau Seven'. When Speer and Schirach were released on 30 September 1966, Hess remained the prison's sole inmate for the next 21 years. Following his death it was demolished to prevent it becoming a neo-Nazi shrine.

The legacy

The trial of the prominent leaders of Nazi Germany had lasted 218 days, 236 witnesses had been questioned in total and 5,330 documents and 200,000 statements had been submitted as evidence. The possibility of conducting further trials of Nazi war criminals had already been discussed earlier in 1946, but there was little will for a repeat performance on a similar scale.

There was a more pressing issue. Tensions between the Soviet Union and the West were now escalating at a rapid pace, making the likelihood of any further co-operation quite impossible.

Representatives of the world's press dash off with news of the sentences meted out to the accused.

However, this did not spell the end of the Nuremberg story. The aim of the Tribunal was not only to bring 22 prominent National Socialist leaders to justice, but also to indict the official groups and organizations through which these men had been able to function. The Allied Control Council – the four-power authority that governed Germany and Austria after the war – had provided a mechanism that enabled any of the occupying authorities to try suspected war criminals in their own respective zones. As a result, the United States would hold a further 12 trials in Nuremberg, this time manned wholly by United States judges and prosecutors. These so-called 'Subsequent Nuremberg Trials' began in December 1946 with 23 Nazi physicians and concluded a year later when 14 Nazi High Command generals were prosecuted.

The Nuremberg Trials would play a significant role in the future of international law, but they had not been without their critics. The most common complaint to be levelled at them was that they were merely a more polished form of 'victors' justice' – or as US Chief Justice Harlan Fiske Stone called it, 'a high-grade lynching party'. One of his colleagues, William O. Douglas, described them as 'unprincipled ... created ex post facto to suit the clamour of the time'. Of course, if charges truly were carried out based wholly on violations of existing laws and agreements then that argument could not possibly hold water. Yet it was true that not all of the Axis powers had been signatories to all of the treaties and agreements, perhaps bringing into question some of the judgements relating to war crimes and crimes against humanity.

When reading through some of the shocking details within the transcripts of the Nuremberg Trials, however, it's certainly easy to view such arguments as quibbling over the fine print. It is simply impossible not to be affected by the harrowing descriptions of these events. Whatever we may think about their fairness or the manner in which the Nuremberg Trials were conducted, or wherever we might stand on the morality of capital punishment, one simple fact remains. Some of the most appalling crimes in human history were perpetrated during 12 years of Nazi rule in Germany. And the international community agreed that somebody had to be held to account for those crimes.

Index